Crossing the Plains

New Harmony, Indiana
to
Camptonville, California

*The Diary
of
Mary Alexander Casey Variel*

As Collected by William J. Variel, Her Son

Edited by Stephanie Korney

Copyright © 2015 Camptonville Historical Society

All rights reserved.

ISBN 1491248769

DEDICATION

To the Camptonville Pioneers

Joshua Hutchings Variel & Mary Alexander Casey Variel

Wedding Portrait, 1848

CONTENTS

Introduction

1 Preparations and Beginnings 9

2 Cholera 25

3 Rivers and Forts 31

4 Into California 47

5 Garden Valley 53

6 Camptonville 59

7 The Variel Family 69

8 Maps 79

9 Notes 91

10 Illustrations 105

INTRODUCTION

In 1852, Mary Alexander Variel left her home in Indiana and embarked on the long journey to the California gold fields with her husband and two children. The Variels were as prepared as they could be to make the trip, and as her diary shows, Mary managed to keep her spirits up most of the time. However, the hardships of the trail are hard to underestimate, as is the nature of the trail. Pioneers faced heat, cold, dust, hunger, thirst, sickness and death with every step and had to travel as quickly as possible to get to California before winter came to the mountains. The sheer number of emigrants from the East is staggering to consider. Most used the route that became known as the California/Oregon Trail.

The year 1846 is notable for the tragedy of the Donner-Reed Party, which became stranded in the Sierra Nevadas over the winter due to a late start, a series of unforeseen events, and some bad advice. Leaving aside their terrible experience, about 1,400 emigrants made the journey across the plains successfully in that year, most in search of gold.

John Sutter emigrated to California in 1839 and his discovery of gold in 1848 set off one of the largest migrations of settlers in history. By the time the Gold Rush ended in1853, an estimated 250,000 travelers had made the journey along the California Trail.

There were other travel options. Some decided to go ship around the tip of South America. Others crossed the Isthmus of Panama. Most gold-seekers, however, found the land route across the country on the Trail to be the safest and cheapest way to get west.

California emigrants faced the greatest challenges of all the pioneer emigrants of the mid-19th century. In addition to the Rockies, these emigrants faced the barren deserts of Nevada and the imposing Sierra Nevada Range. Unlike other pioneers of the day, many of the Forty-Niners were ill-prepared for the journey. [1]

At Fort Laramie, the final stop before climbing the Rocky Mountains, most travelers had to lighten their loads and discarded many of their possessions along the trail. In July 1849, John D. Lee set out from Salt Lake City going east on the California Trail. He returned within a month awed by what he had seen.

> *"The road was so lined with wagons... That one would be scarcely ever out of sight of some train. Dust very disagreeable, but not to compare with the stench from dead carcasses which lie along the road, having died from fatigue and hunger. Destruction of property along the road was beyond description, consisting of wagons, harness, tools of every description, provisions, clothing, stoves, cooking vessels, powder, lead, and almost everything, etc. that could be mentioned."* [2]

William Swain of Youngstown, New York wrote to his brother and wife about his journey to the gold fields in 1849.

---

[1] Dary, David, *The Oregon Trail: An American Saga*. Alfred A. Knopf, New York 2004
[2] Ward, Geoffrey C. and Dayton Duncan, *The West: An Illustrated History*. Little, Brown, Boston, 1996

> *"There is some talk between us of your coming to this country" Swain wrote to his brother. "For God's sake think not of it. Stay at home. Tell all whom you know that are thinking of coming that they have to sacrifice everything and face danger in all forms, for George, thousands have laid and will lay their bones along the routes to and in this country."* [3]

Cholera was epidemic on the Gold Rush trail and killed many travelers on the steamers even before they got to the trail's jumping-off point in Missouri. Others died on the way to Fort Laramie. Few outbreaks occurred past the fort, however. While the exact number of cholera deaths is not known, the St. Louis Republican newspaper estimated that there was one death for every mile-and-a-half of the trip from the Missouri River to Fort Laramie.[4]

Many pioneers joked about having "seen the elephant." This was a common phrased used to suggest that the individual had experienced the hard and difficult journey along the California Trail. The expression may have its origin in a story about a farmer going to town to sell his produce and see a circus elephant. On the way, the farmer encountered the traveling circus and the elephant, the sight of which spooked his horse who ran away, dumping the vegetables. The farmer replied, "But I don't give a hang, for I have seen the elephant." [5]

---

[3] Ward, Geoffrey C. and Dayton Duncan, *The West: An Illustrated History*. Little, Brown, Boston, 1996.

[4] Dary, David, *The Oregon Trail: An American Saga*. Alfred A. Knopf, New York 2004

[5] Levy, JoAnn and Henry Mace, *Women in the Goldrush*. 2004. 3ww.goldrush.com/~joann/elephant.htm

In spite of the hardships and setback, about 40,000 men entered California in 1849, over half of them in their 20s... In 1849, a pioneer woman remarked, "It would astonish you to see of the number of people going to California. It would be the greatest sight you ever saw. The people are of all kinds, some of the first people in the United States are a-going and some of the meanest are also along." [6]

The California Trail began at various jumping-off points in Missouri such as St. Joseph and Independence. The specific route that emigrants and Forty-Niners used depended on their starting point in Missouri, their final destination in California, the condition of their wagons and livestock, and yearly changes in water and forage along the different routes.

The trail passed through Missouri, Kansas, Nebraska, Colorado, Wyoming, Idaho, Utah, Nevada, Oregon, and California Many new routes were opened into California as a result of the Gold Rush. With an estimated 140,000 emigrants arriving in California via the California Trail between 1849 and 1854, routes were continually modified, tested or even abandoned.

The U.S. National Park Service lists the central cutoffs and alternate routes on the trail and the dates on which they began to be used, as:[7]

1844   Sublette Cutoff

1846   Hastings Cutoff

---

[6] Olson, James C. *History of Nebraska*. University of Nebraska Press, Lincoln. 1966
[7] *"The California Trail, Digging In: Trails of Nebraska*
http://cdrh.unl.edu/diggingin/trailsummaries/di.sum.0007.html

1848	Salt Lake Cutoff
1849	Hudspeth Cutoff
1850	Childs Cutoff
1850	Kinney Cutoff
1850	Seminole Cutoff
1850	Slate Creek Cutoff
1852	Baker-Davis Road
1856	Dempsey-Hockadsy Cutoff
1858	Lander Road
1859	Julesburg Cutoff
1859	Western routes include:
1844	Truckee Route
1846	Applegate Trail
1848	Carson Route
1848	Lassen Route
1851	Beckwourth Trail
1852	Nobles Road
1852	Sonora Road

By 1853, the Gold Rush came to a close. However, home seekers continued steady use of the California Trail. With an estimated 250,000 travelers, the California Trail was the most frequented trail in the west.[8]

Part of the California Trail was known as the Great Platte River Road. The Platte River had many channels and islands.

---

[8] Olson, James C. *History of Nebraska*. *University of Nebraska Press, Lincoln*. *1966*

It was shallow, crooked and muddy, and even canoes could not travel very far along its course. The river's valley did provide a relatively easy road for wagons to use, and its direction was almost due west. The river valley offered access to water, forage for the oxen, the possibility of buffalo meat and hides, and the "buffalo chips" the pioneers used to fuel their fires. The Platte was about one mile wide and had a depth that ranged from two inches to 60 inches. The water was full of silt, but if no other water was available, it could be used after letting it sit in a bucket for an hour to allow the silt to settle.

Some Forty-Niners crossed the South Platte before continuing up to the North Platte to Fort Laramie in present-day Wyoming. After crossing over the South Platte the travelers encountered Ash Hollow with its steep descent down Windlass Hill. They would pass large rock formations: Courthouse Rock, Chimney Rock, Castle Rock, and Scotts Bluff.

Prior to 1852 those on the river's north side ferried or used a toll bridge across the North Platte to the south side and Fort Laramie. After 1852, they generally used Child's Cutoff to stay on the north side until they reached a point where they could most easily cross to the south side.

The road west of Fort Laramie was much rougher because of the many streams that fed the North Platte cut the earth into numerous hills and ravines. The river in this area was often located in a deep canyon, and the road moved away from it. Sallie Hester, an 1850 traveler on the road, described the terrain as something clawed by a gigantic bear with "sixty miles of the worst road in the world." From Omaha,

Nebraska, the Platte and North Platte were followed for about 650 miles to Casper in Wyoming. The waters flowed faster after Fort Laramie, minimizing the danger of cholera, and deaths from the disease dropped significantly.

In her diary, Mary describes in a very personal way the nature of the trail and the experience of its many dangers and hardships, bringing the journey to life.

MARY ALEXANDER VARIEL

I

PREPARATIONS AND BEGINNINGS

"Oh, California, California
Is the land for me,
I'm going to California
With my washbowl on my knee.

When I get to California
I will look all around,
I'll see the great big gold lumps
And pick them off the ground.

Oh, California, California
Is the land for me,
I'm going to California
With my washbowl on my knee."

The above lines are all that I recall of a song that I heard sung for the first time in New Harmony, Indiana, in 1848. It appears to have been a product of the excitement attending the discovery of gold in California. Some enthusiastic miner with the poetic fervor had in this manner given expression of the faith that was within him, and at the same time had put in concise form a suggestion of the greatest possibilities in the golden State of California for the one seeking fortune. I heard the song a great deal at the time mentioned, and I recall that it made a great impression on me.

New Harmony, Indiana, circa 1850

It was first sung to my sister and myself, as I stated, in 1848, by a young man by the name of John Wesley Cox, who was enthusiastic to go to California, but who, so far as I know, never realized his golden dream. I was about to be married at this time, and I remember that my intended husband and myself had many very earnest talks about going out to California after our marriage.

I was married on October 21, 1848, to Joshua Hutchings Variel. My husband and I were greatly interested in the inducements that a trip to California offered, and while we frequently discussed the possibilities of such a venture, we were thoroughly alive to and considered fully the toil, danger and uncertainty that would attend it, but countless stories of the boundless gold fields where we could go out with a basket and pick up a supply of gold nuggets at any time overcame any fears we had entertained, and we concluded to join the first expedition that was organized in our neighborhood.

I might say here that my husband was born in East Minot, Cumberland County, Providence of Maine, in 1816, and he was the eldest of a family of thirteen children. He left home in 1836 and with two or three companions "pioneered" across what were then the wilds of Maine, New Hampshire, Vermont, New York, Ohio, Indiana and Illinois, traveling in an old barouche drawn by two horses. He was under contract with a man by the name of Grosvener to buy furs and skins from the Indians. He led this life of a trader for several years and then settled at the little town of New Harmony, Indiana, near where I was born.

The few years he spent as a trader naturally developed a spirit of adventure in him, and the discovery of gold on the far Pacific Coast fired his ambition. As stated, we determined to make the venture, but our plans did not fully develop until three years later.

Some of our neighbors, who had been out to California, had brought some gold nuggets which were shown us, and they told the most alluring stories of the great gold diggings and of the enormous fortunes that had been made and were being made. Other neighbors had gone to California and had sent back for their wives and children. All of these things greatly excited us and fired our enthusiasm, and we looked about among our neighbors for recruits.

By the fall of 1851 a plan had been fully matured for a journey across the plains with ox teams, and orders were at once placed by the heads of families who were interested in the trip for the construction of big, strong ox wagons. While these wagons were being built, the "men folks" were busily engaged in purchasing oxen, "breaking them in" and training them to the yoke, and collecting the necessary tools, implements, and supplies for the journey, while the "women folks" busied themselves in laying in supplies of medicine and the many little delicacies and necessaries that only a woman would think of and of which a man would never dream.

Each family furnished its own oxen, wagon, and supplies, and if any outsider desired to join the expedition, he could do so by paying one hundred dollars cash for the privilege, the money to go into a common fund, and he in consideration thereof to have food and shelter and the protection of the rest of the parties, and in addition to the money paid, was to do his share of the work on the journey in making and breaking camp, driving team, and standing guard at night while we were in the Indian country.

By the latter part of March, 1852, all arrangements had been completed, and the start was actually made about the 11th of April, from New Harmony, Indiana. A portion of our party had gone overland across Illinois to Saint Joe, Missouri, two weeks before, and they were to await our arrival at that point.

It was a bright, beautiful Sunday morning about the 11th of April that that portion of the expedition to go by steamer to Saint Joe started from New Harmony to go to Evansville on the Ohio River. We had three large wagons, each drawn by four "yoke" or eight oxen, and about thirty people made up the party.

We arrived at Evansville after two days' travel, and then bought some supplies and without much delay we got all of our effects and ourselves on board the steamer — wagons, oxen, supplies, men, women, and children — and when the last goodbyes were said, and they were sad and tearful ones, our steamer, the "Brooklyn," swung out into the current and then down the broad Ohio, and we were actually on our journey.

Evansville, Indiana

As I recall it, everybody in our party seemed light-hearted. We expected to be gone only two years, that being the time within which everybody was supposed to pick up gold enough for any use, and then we were to return home.

Two years! Home! Fortune! I wonder how many of that band of thirty actually did make his or her fortune in the Golden State? Not one, I believe, and none of the party returned within the time set, and most of them never did return. Vain hopes of youth!

I was quite enthusiastic and quite willing to make the trip, and although I endured many hardships and passed through many dangers and did not pick up many of the big gold nuggets that the old song suggested might be lying around (although I gathered a few) somehow I never, either during the journey or since, regretted taking the trip I did.

We were to steam down the Ohio, thence up the Mississippi to the mouth of the Missouri, thence up the Missouri to "Saint Joe," Missouri, where we were to join the rest of our party, who had preceded us overland, and then to go into camp until the final arrangements were made for the real start across the desert. Our vessel was a very old side-wheel river steamer, and was commanded by Captain Duff, a gallant young officer who had with him his young wife and their one-year-old child. The captain was kind and considerate, and extended to his passengers every courtesy possible.

I wore the badge of a Daughter of Rebecca (Independent Order of Odd Fellows), having become a member of a chapter of that society in New Harmony. The badge consisted of a green, pink and white ribbon worn about the neck, ending in a bow. The captain was a member of the Odd Fellows, and my badge at once attracted his attention, and it no doubt was the means of my children and myself receiving many a little favor that we otherwise would have missed.

This I appreciated very much, and if it hadn't been for his kindness I do not know how I should have gotten along. It was a rather serious undertaking on my part to have the care of a little three-year-old son and a six-months-old daughter; besides rendering to others assistance when called on to do so.

The trip down the Ohio was a very pleasant outing. We had music and singing, and in the evening two fiddlers furnished music for regular old-time dances, in which most of the passengers indulged. Everyone seemed light-hearted and none appeared to be worrying over, or to realize the dangers or hardships, or labor in store for us.

If we had realized then what was ahead of us, I believe Captain Duff would have been compelled to turn back and return us all to Evansville. I supposed, though, that it was the prize of golden nuggets that were awaiting our baskets that lured us on, for we did not turn back, and never thought of doing so.

Nothing worthy of note happened during our journey down the Ohio, as the river was clear and smooth, and when we turned from the Ohio and steamed up the broad Mississippi, we still had pleasant traveling. The great river was comparatively smooth and, as I remember it, the water was fairly clear. We arrived at St. Louis (Missouri), on a Saturday night after our run from Evansville, but we did not go ashore until the next day.

As the boat came to her moorings at the river bank, a dance was in progress, and some men on the shore started to come aboard, but they were prevented from doing so by some of our men calling out "There is smallpox on this boat." This had the desired effect, for no one attempted to come on board that night, and the dance went on.

The next day was Sunday, and we could not buy anything at the stores, they all being closed, and so we had to wait until the next day. The Monday following, our men purchased the supplies that were to furnish us with food during our journey, as no food at all was brought from home except some delicacies in the way of preserves and pickles that I had brought.

The buying and loading of supplies was completed by Monday evening, and during the night we once more set out up the Mississippi, turning into the muddy Missouri river when we reached its mouth.

St. Louis Levee

Our journey on the steamboat thus far had been without any incident worth relating, but when we reached the Missouri, our troubles commenced. The river was rough and turbulent, and contained many sunken logs, and one day while we were carefully steaming our way up the stream, it was our misfortune to run into one of these. I was terrified by feeling the boat give a sudden lurch, and then to hear the pilot's voice ring out: "Everybody on deck! The boat is on a snag!"

Everybody rushed out on deck and the little steamer seemed to be fairly standing on her stern. Her bow was up in the air and it was with great difficulty that I was able to stand up on the deck. The pilot stood in the pilot house, his face pale as death. In a few minutes the boat righted herself, and the pilot's cheery cry of "All's clear," quieted our fears and restored our equanimity.

It appeared that fortune was with us, for we were told by the Captain that if the accident had occurred in the night time, we would all probably have been lost, but the blessed daylight, enabling the officers to properly handle their boat, saved us. My husband fell on the deck during the confusion and sprained his ankle quite severely, which injury bothered him throughout the journey; in fact, he never did get over it, as he ever after had a weak ankle.

A day later we had another accident that might have proven very serious. We were steaming along very close to the shore early in the morning while we were seated at breakfast. I happened to look out of the door towards the stern and saw a big blaze going up from a wagon in that part of the boat. The sight of it filled me with terror.

I said nothing, but acted very quickly. I quietly picked up my two little children and walked out of the cabin. By the time I reached the side of the steamer she had stopped and the bell was loudly clanging the fire alarm. Some of the deck hands had hastily thrown out the gang plank to the river bank, and this I lost no time in mounting with my two little children in my arms. As I walked away from the river I could hear the loud voices of men calling out, and the screams of women and children.

In a few minutes the fire was put out and quiet restored, and I returned to the boat. It appeared that in some way a feather bed had got on fire and for a few moments it looked very serious for us, but the only effect of it was a terrible fright, and that was so great that the boat remained at her moorings for a couple of hours before proceeding up the river.

I was very much frightened, of course, but I kept my nerve, and made up my mind to get to a place of safety as quickly as possible, at least a place that was safe from the fire, and land seemed to me at the time to be about the safest place. It did not occur to me at the time what in the world I should have done there alone in that wilderness with my children, if the boat had burned up.

We proceeded up the river and arrived in due time at Saint Joe, Missouri, after a seventeen days' run from Evansville. This steamer trip was not as pleasant as it might have been, and possibly the many years gone by have somewhat softened the recollection of the hardships, and perhaps my remembrance is not of the best, but the note which I find my husband made in his diary of the event is as follows:

The best place on the river is Saint Joe. This is a pleasant town (save when the wind blows and then it is disagreeable) of some 2500 inhabitants, and is backed by some of the finest country that I ever saw, and some of it is well cultivated. We arrived here on the last day of April, after the most tedious trip I ever took in any way, for to be cooped up in an old rotten and filthy boat seventeen days is bad, but to be thus situated and then put on half rations is truly remarkable, but such was our fate.

St. Joseph, Missouri

Personally, my trip on the steamer was not a pleasant one on account of the selfishness of some of the women in our party, and the first night on the boat I had to sleep on the cabin floor, but after that time I was able to share one of the cabins with two other ladies. Our party lost no time in disembarking with wagons, cattle and supplies, and at once joined the rest of our party who had come overland and had arrived there three days previously.

We harnessed our ox-teams, four yoke of oxen to each wagon, loaded on our supplies, and drove our teams to the ferry boat, and were ferried over to the other side of the river, and then drove out about two miles from the river, where our friends had established a camp. My husband was greatly incensed at the treatment I had received at the hands of the other women. I will quote from his diary describing the landing at Saint Joe:

I am sorry to have to say it, but the Harmony women treated my family in anything but a respectful manner, and oftentimes with open insult. As usual, those upon whom we have the least claims showed us the most kindness, and to crown all, when we landed, I had to check off our freight, and all the other hands had nothing to do but get their things, which they did by pulling up and leading their wagons. This occupied all the forenoon.

During all this time my family had to remain on the bank in the hot sun and dirt, and no one offered my wife a place in their wagon, nor even spoke to her, except to quarrel with her for things she could not help, and when they got loaded, I asked Mr. P. to let my family ride out to camp in his wagon, but he had no room, and the other teams drove off under 'J.C.'s' directions and left us standing on the bank of the river, to get out to camp as best we could, but ingratitude is always punished, and in this case it was instant, for he let 'M.C.'s' team run against his wagon and smashed one hind wheel to atoms, but I did not follow his course towards me. I went and borrowed a wheel and helped him to start, and we finally got out to camp and pitched our tents before dark. This was the first day of May.

The same day, just after we arrived in camp, the pilot of the steamer, whose name I cannot remember, came into the camp carrying his "carpet sack," and told us that the steamer had sunk. On returning to the river, there, sure enough, we saw only the pilot house of the old "Brooklyn" above the water.

I then for the first time realized what a peril we had passed through on the trip, as I learned from that pilot that the boat was a rotten old craft, and that she had been greatly overloaded, and that we had really taken great chances in making the voyage in her.

Many of us thought at the time that from the fact that the

boat was so heavily insured, that she was sunk on purpose to get the insurance — I have been told that that was a common practice in those days.

Everybody was busy now dividing stores and packing wagons. The notes in my husband's diary shed some light on the trials and difficulties attending the few days of our final preparations:

Today I have determined to have another team or stop at Saint Joe. M.C. and I bought Z. Johnson's half of a team, consisting of a wagon and outfit and two yoke of oxen, and I now have Cuddy for a partner.

We moved this team out to the camp and I set up for myself. May 4, 5, 6, 7 and 8 were occupied in fitting out, and for me it is very unpleasant, for there is but one who left Harmony who is disposed to see me have a fair chance. Mr. C. has done all that he could, and has acted the man. We have got our team now of four yoke of oxen.

May 8. Today we have divided our stores, and I will say with truth that I never knew the definition of selfish before, but now I can appreciate it in its fullest sense, but cannot tell all the little mean things I saw it do, and would like to forget it. Truly is this the place to try men.

May 9. Today, Sunday, we broke up camp and moved up to the ferry four miles above Saint Joe, and camped for the night.

May 10. Today was spent in fixing wagons and in the evening, we crossed the river in a hard rain storm, and ascended the bluff, which is a very bad hill of some two hundred feet in height, with a grade of forty degrees. It was so wet that we had to put twelve yoke of oxen (twenty-four animals) to a wagon, and hard work at that. But we go up safely, minus the breaking of a few chains and cracking P's whip stock of hoosier oak. We camped one and a quarter miles from the Missouri, where we found good grass and a good spring of water.

May 11. We are now fairly afloat and our destiny is westward. All well and in good spirits, except Mr. P. who has been unwell with d-- for several days, but is too cross to be in any danger

While in camp we were visited by Indians, who exacted from every man a toll of one dollar for the privilege of going through their country. And we had to pay 25 cents for each wagon every time we crossed a bridge. They were very friendly, were well dressed and could speak very good English, they having lived near the town of Saint Joe. There were the Kickapoo Indians.

When our preparations were all completed and the start was actually made, our "emigrant train," as it was called in those days, was made up of eleven large wagons, or prairie schooners, covered with canvas, each drawn by four yoke, or eight oxen, and our emigrant company consisted of about fifty people, men women, and children, and of course, a few of man's best friend, our faithful dogs.

I cannot recall the names of the entire party, but those I do remember are the following:

J.H. Variel and wife, Mrs. Mary Alexander Variel, and their two children, the one then three years old being the late Hon. R.H. F. Variel of Los Angeles, and the other, a daughter, six months old, who is now Mrs. Bell C. Eaton of Ventura County; Michael Craddock and Jane Craddock, his wife; Henry Hugo, fifteen years old; Mrs. Corbin and Tiny Corbin, her two-year-old daughter, going to join her husband; Daniel Perky; William Galloway; Monis Burbeck; Charles Twigg; Frank McNear; Charles Pritchard; Mrs. James Budden and her three daughters, Kate, Mary, Lily, aged sixteen, nine and seven years (going to join her husband in California who was out there practicing medicine); Burt Kellogg; -- Cuddy; Frank Durlin; J. Dunn with his wife and baby; Henry Hall; John and Mark Delaney; "French Louis" (cook); Thomas Cox and wife; George Grant, wife and sisters; Fidelia Lyon (her husband was in Nevada City, and she was going on to join him); Green Cox; William Davis, wife and baby; William Bradley; Zummerich McFadden; ----Racquet; "Sid"----; Henry Ivens, an eleven-year-old boy; and Zark Johnson.

When we started we had a fine watch dog, and I got a great deal of comfort by having him, as he was always about watching over my children.

Early Emigrant Train

The first Indians we saw, as previously stated, were at our first camp near Saint Joe, they being "tame Indians." They very promptly made demands on us to pay "toll," and of course, we had nothing else to do but pay it, and this put them in a good humor. They had a big camp fire near us and the old chief came over and invited me to go over to their fires and warm my tea, but having a little iron stove for that purpose, I declined his invitation.

I gave my little son, Robert, fifty cents to give to the chief, the latter having inspired the child with a very wholesome fear, but he walked up to the old fellow and said, "Here, four bits."

The chief took the coin and bowed very low, and again invited us to his camp, but I declined.

In making the final arrangements for our overland trip, we chose one of the men as captain, Mr. M. Craddock, but my husband and another man were chosen lieutenants and had a good deal to say about the conduct of affairs. It was arranged that two men should in rotation stand guard each night and watch our cattle, two staying up until midnight, and two others the balance of the night.

We also arranged our mode of travel and making camp. Each wagon took its turn in leading, and when the captain in the evening ordered a halt for camp, the first wagon would take a position so that that it would be the last one to move the next morning, and then the other wagons as they came up would fall in position, the wagons when all had halted being in a circle, forming a circular barricade or fort, inside of which we pitched our tents and built our individual camp fires.

Wagons Crossing the Plains

In the back end of our wagon my husband had built an excellent pantry, which was very tight and in which I kept supplies for immediate use in very good shape. Each wagonload and party had its own supplies, and did its own cooking, there being no community interest in this respect.

We had tin plates, tin cups, iron knives and forks, and our eatables consisted of tea, coffee, sugar, crackers, flour, hams, shoulders, smoked bacon and cheese.

We had no canned goods, as this was before the era of that very convenient form of food. I had bought two bushels of dried peaches before we started, and this furnished us with what seemed at the time a very delicious dessert during the entire journey.

I did all of the cooking for our wagon party, consisting of my husband, two children and myself, and two men, "Cuddy" and Louis," both Frenchmen. Louis always gathered the fuel, carried water and washed the dishes for me, little favors that were much appreciated by the cook.

I boiled water every night after supper, and in the morning before starting filled four big canteens and a little one for Robert, with this cooled, boiled water.

By this means our wagon party, at least, always had a good supply of wholesome water, something that some of the others neglected, and to their cost, as will be seen.

We found the road well defined, as it had been marked out and traveled over by the thousands of emigrants who had preceded us on their way to the gold fields. We generally traveled about twenty miles each day, the country for the first hundred miles being quite level.

II

CHOLERA

One evening just as we had reached our camping place and had prepared for the night, we learned that John Craddock, brother of our Captain, had been taken quite ill with a complaint something like cholera. This was undoubtedly brought on by his drinking unboiled water. The poor man came to my wagon and told me that he was very sick and that he believed he had the cholera, and asked me for some "pain killer."

I got out our bottle of patent medicine and handed it to him, telling him to take six drops of it in a tumbler of water, every hour or so. I offered to mix up the medicine for him, but he looked at the bottle a moment, and instead of following my direction, he placed it to his lips and commenced drinking it straight.

I cried out, "Don't drink it that way, it will kill you," but he drank down the entire contents of the bottle, and after smacking his lips, he remarked, "Well, if six drops would help me, I guess the whole bottle will do me more good."

He turned and walked to his wagon, and I heard nothing more of him until about midnight that night, when I was startled from my slumber by his wife crying out to me to let her have some of my brandy. She was terribly excited and scared and said, "I do believe my husband is dying of the cholera, he is all doubled up."

I gave her the brandy, but he was too far gone, and died within an hour. It was a cold, dismal night, and the wind blew a fierce gale. They dropped the tent right over his dead body and went to bed, leaving the corpse without watchers.

We laid by the next day and night, and during the day we buried the last mortal remains of the first victim, burying it at the foot of a beautiful granite boulder. This rock had red streaks in it and we called it "Calico Rock." The body was sewed up in a blanket (for a coffin was out of the question) and let down into a grave about four feet deep and was then covered up, no ceremony of any kind being had.

It was a mournful affair, and we all felt very much depressed, each one no doubt wondering who would be called next. Our fear of cholera was not ill-founded, for we had just passed another emigrant train that had four bad cases of cholera. After recuperating for the day and night following the death of our comrade, we continued our westward journey.

One morning while I was walking along ahead of the front wagon to escape the dust (for I, in fact, walked most of the way across the plains in this way), I all but stepped on the body of a dead man lying near the road. It was that of a white man, and the body was only half covered with earth. One arm was bare and protruded from the shallow and hastily made grave. The body appeared to have been only recently buried, and some of us thought that the poor fellow had been buried alive as the position of the body would indicate this, for it certainly could not have been buried with one arm sticking out. The suggestion was horrible.

Death on the Trail

He had probably died of cholera. In the cholera scourges, many people were buried in such haste that life oftentimes was not extinct. Our men, however, finished the burial for they took their spades and covered the body.

We traveled on, and two nights after the death of John Calloway, Sarah, John's sister, was taken down sick with cholera. We stopped on account of the sick woman, and did what we could to alleviate her sufferings. She was a good, kind-hearted woman, and my heart went out to her. She had a nine-months' old baby, and the prospect of this little child being left an orphan was terrible.

The poor woman lay sick all day, and I went to her and found her lying on a board in her tent. She was very sick and suffered great pain. She told me she was sure she was going to die, but I spoke to her encouragingly and set about trying to do something for her.

She was very cold so I got some rocks heated up and put them to her feet and gave her hot pepper tea; she seemed to get better, but she was terribly frightened and kept crying that she didn't want to die and be buried in a blanket.

Her brother's death and burial had terrified her, and I believe that if her courage could have been kept up, she would have recovered. She kept crying that she was going to die and during the evening became very low, and just about midnight her terrified, troubled soul passed away.

The night, though clear, was very cold, as it had been raining during the day, and a fierce wind was blowing that chilled to the bone. The sky was slightly overcast, and black clouds shifted rapidly across the face of the pale moon.

We were all terror-stricken at the death of our friend, and a deep gloom pervaded the camp. Most of the camp were up and about, each one, no doubt, filled with his or her own thoughts of loneliness and sorrow.

I walked over to the tent of the dead woman just a few moments after she died, and was about to go into the tent to assist the other ladies in preparing the body for burial, when I was started and fairly transfixed by a loud, long, unearthly scream issuing from some bushes nearby.

It sounded like a woman screaming out in agonized terror, and at the same time it had the fierceness and power that betokened some powerful wild animal. It was terrible, and I was frightened half to death. It was so strange and weird, too, at that lonely midnight hour when death had just claimed a victim, for that panther to be at our camp and give out that terrible cry. I have often wondered about it since.

I have never heard a dog howl at night since, that I haven't recalled that panther's scream. It is said that dogs howl when a human soul passes away. What relation was there possibly between the death of our poor friend that dismal night, and the one dreadful scream of that panther? It was evidently a strange coincidence, and such a thing as would be calculated to fill us all with superstitious dread. I know I did not sleep any that night, and I doubt if anybody in camp slept, and a close watch was had at the tent of death.

We laid by another day to bury the dead. This solemn duty having been performed, we spent the rest of the day in altering our tents, sunning our clothes and doctoring the sick. After that it was westward again.

A night of two after Sarah died, another of our party, Charles Twigg, was taken sick with cholera. He had been a friend and neighbor at New Harmony, and I felt very kindly towards him, so when I learned that he was sick, I determined to make an effort to save him. He had great confidence in me and begged me to do something for him.

I heated a board over the fire and made my husband put it on the sick man's stomach, and ordered it to be kept there hot, and made him drink a quart of hot milk in which I had sprinkled a generous quantity of red cayenne pepper.

He soon showed marked improvement, he sweat very freely, and the severe pains he had been suffering left him, and he slept all night and the next morning rode in his wagon, and by another day or two he was well. He always said that I saved his life.

The next day still another member of our party, Rall

McFadden, was taken ill with the same trouble. Twigg came to me at once and said, "Get your milk and pepper and hot board, Mrs. Variel. McFadden is down sick."

I pursued the same course of treatment with him as with Twigg, and in addition gave him some hot brandy and he got well in a couple of days. After this, I was called "Doctor," and I was soon summoned "professionally" to the tent of Charley Pritchard, who a few days later was taken down with the same dread disease. I gave him the same treatment and he got well in a few days, though he, as well as the others, had to ride in a wagon several days while we were traveling, on account of being so weak.

Walking across the Plains

Let me remark here that no man was allowed to ride at any time unless ill, he being compelled to walk all the way across the plains, and we women, too, walked in the aggregate, many hundreds of miles, for we preferred to walk ahead to escape the dust, and it was about as easy to walk as to ride in those big, lumbering, "dead ax" wagons.

The treatment I used I had learned from my mother, and I gave them the benefit of this "home remedy." I insisted, though, that nobody should drink any water that was unboiled, and told them they would all die if they didn't boil their drinking water. This admonition was very scrupulously observed by everyone after that, and we, in fact, had no more serious illness in our party.

III

RIVERS AND FORTS

We crossed many rivers in our travels, but there was one in particular, some two hundred miles west of Saint Joe, where there was a ferry and we had to pay $1.50 per wagon to get ferried over. There was, also, a store at this point where we got a few supplies, but were compelled to pay outrageous prices. The man who kept this store, I understood from my husband, dealt largely in whiskey and so-called brandy, and some of our men got a taste of the stuff, and it did not do them any good, either.

A Kansas Ferry

Our oxen were bothered a great deal by great swarms of black bugs; they were in shape and color like the pinch bugs and annoyed our cattle so much one evening that we had a stampede of our oxen and it took the men over an hour to gather them again.

We had many reports from discouraged, returning travelers whom we met, of very short grass and plenty of Indians ahead. This was not very cheering to us, but we kept on. A few miles on from the ferry we met the overland stage, and those who had any letters for home, sent them on.

We reached the Platte River about June 1st; here was Fort Kearny. It was a fine, bright morning when we came in sight of the fort. The soldiers were out parading and it was a very welcome sight, for reports of Indians had made us feel a little nervous. There were three or four frame houses, a few pieces of cannon, and some sixty soldiers, but we saw no American flag.

View of Fort Kearny

We camped a few miles below the fort for noon. Here one of the men deserted or left our party; he quit because he did not like the idea of working. We wrote some letters and mailed them here at the fort. There were no women here, at least I saw none. We did not remain at the fort, but went on several miles that afternoon before camping for the night.

Soon after leaving Fort Kearney, we came across a newly made grave. It had a small plank for a head board on which was written, "The Lone Grave. A Young Girl 18 Years." Whose body lay buried there, or what the circumstances of her death were, could only be conjectured by us, who had seen the fatal ravages of cholera.

This lone grave out there in the boundless desert affected all of us, and it was a long time before we could shake off the overpowering and depressing impression. It was one of the many and almost constantly recurring reminders that death was always lurking about us.

We had found thus far plenty of good water and feed for our animals, but fuel became a very serious question for us as long as we were in the prairie region, wood as fuel being out of the question, and for hundreds of miles the only fuel we had and used was buffalo "chips."

United States Geological Survey

Platte River

We reached the Platte River and were compelled to ford it, as it was so broad, through not very deep. We had been advised to provide blocks to raise the wagon beds so as to keep our supplies from becoming wet. My husband had procured the blocks for our wagon, but many of our party were driven to the expedient of using buffalo skulls for blocks.

Only women and children were allowed to ride across, the men being compelled to wade. As the water was up to the hubs of the wheels, generally, it was no easy task getting across. My husband's ankle had been bothering him a great deal, from the accident on the steamer, and in wading this river he gave out and was compelled to ask for help. Mr. Calloway went to his assistance and threw out his long ox whip, the end of which my husband caught and was thus assisted through.

Fording the River

Our wagon was the last to cross, and just as we were about over, I heard a man calling out in a loud, excited voice for help. I looked back and saw a man, woman, and two children in a two-horse, light wagon, following us; one of the horses had just fallen down and was struggling in the water. The man was trying to extricate the animal, and calling loudly for help, saying he would pay well for any assistance rendered. He asked for a yoke of oxen to pull the wagon out of the river.

Our captain refused to allow any oxen of our train to be used, saying that we had all we could do to take care of ourselves, and he ordered us all to drive on, and we had to leave the poor, unfortunate travelers to their fate. We never knew what became of them, but the cries of the woman and the children, and the hoarse calling and swearing of the man haunted me for many a day. They must have perished, for the last I saw of them, they were gradually moving down stream with the current.

After getting across the river we had to stop to take the blocks off the wagon. We then came into what they called the Big Meadows. Wild oats were up higher than the backs of the oxen but the grasshoppers were so bad that the poor oxen couldn't eat.

These frightful insects fairly covered the cattle, they settled over them in immense swarms and the men were kept busy two or three hours keeping the cattle free of this pest.

It was a terrible trial and it seemed strange that the best feed on the trip should have been practically out of the reach of the poor animals by reason of the presence of these insects that were there in myriads. There were millions and millions of them.

Our cattle had to be beaten at every step to make them move, and if every man had not been at hand the cattle certainly would have broken away and stampeded.

I never doubted the stories I read in after years of the devastation of farms out in Kansas and Nebraska by the grasshoppers, and when I read that a farmer's scythe had its edge eaten off by them during the noon hour, I accepted the story as true without question or comment.

Through this country we had to use the greatest care in the use of water, and I sat up every night until after midnight boiling water for the next day and popping corn; popcorn was said to be a prevention of scurvy, and as we had been on a salt meat and pork diet for some time, we consumed great quantities of popcorn, and - well, there was no scurvy in our party.

We covered twenty miles a day through this part of the country, and nearly every day young men, carrying their blankets, came to us asking for something to eat. They had left their own trains and had been getting along the best way they could. I never refused to give any of them food, but many of the other members of our party objected, and I was the subject of frequent abuse for doing what I considered to be my duty in relieving the hungry.

We drove near a lone elm tree that had one big branch to it, and about this time two travelers joined us on foot. They proved to be "Odd Fellows" and our flag attracted them to our wagon. One of the men said, pointing to the tree, "Many a poor driver has been hung to that tree."

They told us of how on many occasions, in various trains, when some driver had offended the rest, that the men would take their tent poles, rig up a scaffold and hang the poor wretch to it, and then dig a grave and bury him.

We heard many such stories of violence on the plains, and we could easily believe them, for these were the times when men took the law into their own hands, and when they did it was short shift for the offender, no matter what defense he might have.

Ash Hollow

As we neared Fort Laramie, we met four young men, driving an eight-ox team coming back from the West. The young men were crying, and we asked them what was the matter, and they replied that they four, with their Captain, who was an older man, had started from Kentucky to go to California; that everything had gone well until the day before we met them, when their "Captain" had been stricken down with cholera, and had died, and they, after burying him, had lost heart and had turned back towards home. They were nearly frantic with grief and disappointment.

I spoke to one of them and said Kentucky was my state (my parents had formerly lived in the old Blue Grass State, and I had a warm place in my heart for any Kentuckian), and asked them to turn back and go on with us, but they were not to be turned from their purpose, and bade us goodbye, and went on towards home. I have often wondered what became of them.

Soon after this Mrs. Corbin and I, while one morning walking ahead of the train, came up with an ox team, four yoke as usual.

The leader, or Captain, was an old man probably seventy years old, by the name of Ayers, and he was accompanied by two young men, and a young Negro woman who did the cooking for the party. Their oxen were standing still, and apparently they had been in trouble of some kind.

The old man asked me if there were any Masons in our party, and I replied that I didn't know of any except Charles Twigg; that nearly all of our menfolk were Odd Fellows.

One of the young men, Jim Johnson, came and spoke to me and said that the old man had had trouble with the train of which they were members, and that their former companions refused to allow them to travel in company with them any longer, and they had been compelled to fall behind.

Jim begged me very earnestly to allow him to join our train, so we waited until our train came up to see what could be done for the waifs. I at once told Charley Twigg that there was a stranger there with the wagon asking for a Mason.

Charley talked with the Missourian a while, and the latter, after considerable talk and parleying among our men, was permitted to join our train and fall in behind and take its turn, and the two young men were to stand watch in turn as our men were doing.

Several days went by without any incident, Jim especially making himself very useful and agreeable to us all. Ayers was afraid to go on alone for fear of the Indians, and was especially afraid of going down the Humboldt River in Nevada. This was his one fear, and he had begged so hard that it was decided to take him in, no matter what kind of a man he was.

One morning Ayers' wagon was at the rear, and Jim had just finished milking their cow, and he came to me with a bucket partly filled with milk, and asked me if I had anything to put the milk in so as to save it, saying that everything in their wagon was filled. I replied that the pantry was closed up, and that I couldn't make any use of it, as the wagon had gone on.

I always stayed behind when the wagon first started, to see that nothing was left behind. Mr. Ayers was standing chatting with me when Jim came up, and I noticed that Ayres had a long bowie knife in his hand.

When I said I had nothing to put the milk in, Jim simply turned it out on the ground, and as quick as a flash old Ayers drew his hand back and struck at Jim, who was near me on the other side, and would have cut him if I had not struck his arm and knocked the knife to the ground. It was all done very quickly, and I believe the old man would have killed him if I had not been there.

I grabbed up the knife and threw it away as far as I could, and said to the boy, "Jim, take my spade and knock his brains out."

Jim picked up the spade and drew it back to strike, but the old man ran to his wagon and got his gun, but the negro girl grabbed the gun from him and told him it was not loaded.

Jim implored me to let him go with our wagon, and asked Ayers to give him his clothes, but Ayres told him to go on, that he couldn't have them. I pleaded with the old man to give him his things, but the old fiend was obdurate and refused. I said, "Jim, come along my husband has plenty of clothes, and you can get along some way."

Jim told Ayers that he had done a great deal for him, and that he (Jim) had driven his, Ayers', team for two hundred miles in Missouri when the officers were pursuing him. The old man hushed up after this, and we went away and left him. Just as we were about to leave, the old man threw Jim's "carpet-bag" on the ground.

Jim told me afterwards that the old man had stolen the colored girl, who was undoubtedly a slave, and that he had then fled from Missouri. Jim went with me and we finally overtook the train, but Ayers never caught up with us. We afterwards saw him farther on.

It appears that he took the Sale Lake Route, and sold his oxen and bought a wagon and horses, and when we saw him he was going along, driving his team of horses and accompanied by the negro girl and dog.

One evening at sundown, a few days before we arrived at Fort Laramie, we had just stopped for the day and were about to camp. Our wagons were arranged in a circle as usual, and most of the men were away from camp driving the cattle away to graze. I had just gotten down from our wagon with my little boy and my little seven-months-old daughter, and was preparing to get our supper.

It was just dark and several camp fires had already been lighted. Charley Twigg and Frank McLean were at their wagon next to ours, and they were the only men about camp at the time.

Suddenly little Robert spoke up and said, "Here comes circus from Harmony. Where's the old clown? I don't want to see the old clown. I'm afraid of him."

I looked up and there before me were eight brawny Indians, each mounted on a fine big horse. They had no rifles but may have had other weapons.

One of them said, "Here, give me your papoose (baby). I want to see your papoose. I swap papoose with you. My squaw has papoose."

I replied that I wanted to keep my own papoose, that every squaw liked her own papoose best. Not wishing to anger him, or show that I was afraid of him, and some way feeling that I had to take some chances in the matter, I handed my little baby daughter up to him, and said, "Here, you hold my baby while I get you some sugar and crackers."

He took the child, and I ran to the back of my wagon and brought a cupful of brown sugar and a handful of crackers and came back and gave each Indian a cracker and poured some of the brown sugar into each one's hand.

When the spokesman of the party received his cracker and sugar, he said something in Indian tongue to his companions and away they went yelling like demons and running their horses at full speed around the outside of our circle of wagons. I was terribly frightened, as I had heard that the Indians like to get white children, to bring them up, and I anxiously waited for them to return.

They stopped after a couple of revolutions about our camp and the chief stopped by my wagon and handed back my baby, and as he did so, pointed up to the flag that was floating on our wagon and he said, "Heap good flag."

It was the flag of the Independent Order of Odd Fellows and we always had one on our wagon. The flag seemed to impress him as being a very important thing, and he looked at it a long time. He asked me for gunpowder, but I told him we didn't have any.

They waited around a few minutes and then all of a sudden the leader turned his horse, gave a terrible yell, and started away from the camp on the dead run, followed by his seven companions, all yelling like demons.

Charley Twigg and McLean had fallen down under their wagon near by and remained there during the entire colloquy. It did not last more than five minutes, but they were the longest five minutes I ever spent in my life. Twigg, after the Indians left, very bravely crawled out from under the wagon and asked why I gave up my child. I answered that I thought it was the best thing to do under the circumstances. It appeared to me, and I told him, that he did not show very much valor on his part in remaining under the wagon while I was parleying with the Indians. It certainly was very funny to see those two men disappear under their wagon, leaving a defenseless woman to treat with those savages all alone.

When the men returned from putting the oxen out to graze, and learned what had taken place, our Captain was very angry because I had given my crackers and sugar away, saying that I would need those crackers and sugar before I got across. I replied that I didn't think we would need either if we were all killed by the Indians.

It was a lonesome, tedious journey plodding along day after day, and week after week, over a rough, rocky and dusty road, through a country mostly desert and inhabited only by wandering tribes of Indians, and no white people except a few traders scattered here and there along the route of travel.

The further west we journeyed, the greater precautions we took for protection against Indians, as returning emigrants whom we met were constantly warning us against them.

We met bands of them every few days, and they were always on the lookout for crackers and sugar, and powder and bullets. We dispensed the first two articles as freely as our supplies would permit, but we never had any of the other to give away.

Fort Laramie, 1849, Sketch by James Wilkins

We arrived one fine morning at Fort Laramie, the western-most outpost of "Uncle Sam," and the stars and stripes floating over the block house, and the soldiers parading was a pleasing sight to us. We felt the security afforded by the soldiers, but when we left the fort behind, we felt that the last tie was broken connecting us with civilization, and we were strictly dependent on ourselves for protection.

We women often walked on far ahead of the wagons, and once while so walking we came up to where there had recently been a camp. When the wagons came up, one of our men looking about found a bloody hatchet and a pool of fresh blood. There were many things left there indicating a hasty departure, and we always felt that there had probably been violence and murder, but the desert had the secret, and it was safe.

We sustained a loss that I felt very keenly. One of our dogs was detected running after some sheep, and although he was not actually caught killing any, still the owners of the sheep insisted that the dog should be killed, and he had to be sacrificed.

My husband, when we reached the mountainous country, used to make long trips off to the side looking for deer and usually brought home some kind of game which was always acceptable.

One evening he returned to camp and reported having had, so he thought, a narrow escape from being killed by Indians. He said that he was going down one side of a ravine on his way to camp and looking across the canyon he saw an Indian suddenly crouch down behind a big rock. He kept on his way, but also kept his eye on that rock as long as he could. He felt that the Indian would probably have shot and scalped him if he hadn't been seen.

As our supplies had diminished, our wagons were really larger than necessary, and my husband sawed off the hind end and shortened up the running gear so that he wagon was only about two-thirds as large as at first and very materially lessened the load for the poor oxen to haul. This shortening up of the wagons became quite general, and very soon every wagon in the train had been cut off. Everybody was anxious to get along as rapidly as possible, and every hundred pounds of weight counted.

We passed two large emigrant trains one noon. Death had visited them and they were engaged in performing the last sad rites over their dead. Several mounds of fresh dirt showed that more than one had passed over the Great Divide in advance.

Soda Springs

We found some other travelers at this point, they having been delayed on account of a woman in their party having fallen into the hot water and been badly scalded. The woman's husband came to me and asked me to go and see his wife. I found that she had been fearfully scalded, and she was in a very critical condition. I felt that I could do nothing for her, much as I wished to, and had to leave her unattended. She died that night.

About three hundred yards away from this boiling spring was a fine soda spring, and we all enjoyed drinking at this wonderful natural soda fountain.

We came through what was called the Rock City. Huge volcanic rocks reared up on all sides, and at a short distance, looked like a little city. On one of these great rocks we found hundreds of names written.

Signatures at the City of Rocks

We reached the Humboldt River (eastern Nevada) at last, and followed it for some two hundred miles being compelled to ford it several times. The river was quite low and there was not the difficulty experienced as in fording the Platte.

It was while going down the Humboldt that we lost "Old Jerry," one of our oxen. He was turned out to graze with the other cattle, and the next morning he was missing. He had probably been driven off by cattle thieves.

We had been warned about the Humboldt River territory as that was considered one of the most dangerous portions of the journey, as the great quantity of underbrush and willows growing in the low lands furnished ambush for Indians. We were lucky, though, in losing nothing but the one ox. We were compelled to hitch the mate of "Jerry" with two other oxen, driving them three abreast.

As I recall it, we saw no Indians along the Humboldt except an occasional old squaw. They were always begging for crackers and sugar, and several times in giving these little luxuries I was rewarded by having a dirty old squaw embrace me. The compensation for the gift was very objectionable, but I endured it rather than offend.

After leaving the Humboldt, we reached a dry alkali desert; there was neither tree nor shrub nor a drop of water in sight. We did not dare to stop at our usual camping hour, but drove on through the entire night through the desert. We had filled up barrels with water, and during the night trip, we portioned out to each ox a goodly portion of water. If it hadn't been for this, I believe some of the cattle would have dropped in their tracks.

By morning we reached water again and we left as though we had been delivered from great danger. We soon came up to some boiling springs. We heard the noise of the boiling water for some distance, and when we arrived at the springs we found that thoughtful travelers before us had left some barrels and these barrels were all filled with good, wholesome water.

The water as it came out of the earth was very bad, but on being boiled, we found it to be very palatable. After filing up every receptacle in the train with water, we refilled the barrels in pursuance of the law of the desert that required that travelers should always leave the barrels filled, so that others following might have the benefit good cool water.

We came to what was called the Devil's Slide. The road was very steep and rough, and the wagons could not be taken down in the usual way. The method pursued was to unhitch all the oxen but one yoke, and then hitch ropes to the rear axle and let the wagons down one at a time, inch by inch. It was a slow process, but the only way that we would ever have gotten along. I left the men to let the wagons down and went down the gorge on foot, carrying my little children. We soon reached the Truckee River and passed out through Truckee Pass into California.

`After this we came to a dry sandy desert. The weather was oppressively hot, the wagon wheels sank deep in the sand, and the poor oxen could hardly get along. We had not been going more than half an hour over this hot, sandy stretch, then one of our oxen, old "Tom" fell down, overcome with the heat. We unyoked him and left him and his mate on the side of the road. They walked along after the train, and by night we brought them through.

About two oxen to every team in our train gave out in the same way that same day, but they were turned loose and allowed to rest and worry along by themselves, and in this way we did not lose an animal.

A yoke of oxen.

IV

INTO CALIFORNIA

When our ox fell down, I jumped out of the wagon with my children and told the men I was going to walk, and so leaving the elder child in the wagon with a canteen of water and a supply of popcorn, I started on ahead along the road, carrying my baby in my arms, wading through the hot, burning sand that came up to my shoe tops. I kept going until I reached the edge of the desert, and this was three 'clock in the afternoon.

The first thing, almost, that I saw on getting across the sand was a stream of fine water flowing along by a grove of beautiful pine trees. How fine it was to get back into the wooded country again! In looking around I saw near the road a large tree loaded down with a purplish red fruit, which, on examination, I found to be wild plums. It seemed strange that the thousands of people who had passed that way should have overlooked that fruit. I suppose it was considered poisonous. I knew the fruit, however, and by the time our train came up in the evening, every plum had been picked.

It is needless to say that we camped at this point, and what a time everybody and every animal had getting plenty of good wholesome water to drink! When my camp fire was started (and we had regular normal fuel once more), those plums were very soon converted into delicious plum sauce that everybody enjoyed. I have often in after years wondered what became of that plum tree. It was probably twelve feet high and looked like the tame plum trees that we had back home. This camping place was a veritable oasis in the desert, and it was with considerable regret that we broke camp the next morning and left for we knew not what. This desert was, I believe, what is now called Sierra Valley and was our first introduction to California.

When we reached this point, more trouble occurred. Our captain had resigned his office, and the train was without a head - it was now everybody for himself. And then the extra men who had acted as helpers and drivers deserted the train.

They claimed that they had been unfairly treated, but I think that they wanted an excuse to start out without further delay to reach the mines. They packed their blankets, took a supply of food, and trudged off, leaving us to get along as best we could, shorthanded.

We lost two other of the oxen and we had but five left, and no one to drive them by my husband, and we had yet several hundred miles to travel.

About this time another of our party, Charley Pritchard, was taken ill with cholera. He had been ailing for several days, but that awful day trudging through the hot desert was too much for him, and that night he took his bunk a very sick man.

He sent word to me that he was sick and begged me to look after him; I promptly applied the "hot board" treatment and gave him fresh hot milk with cayenne pepper in it, and soon had him away from the danger point. It nearly burned him up, he said, but he got better and was able to travel the next day, though of course too weak to walk.

I told him he might ride in my wagon and that I would get out and walk, but Mrs. Budden said he might ride in her wagon with herself and daughters, and there he rode all day, but that night when we halted for camp, the sick man had gotten up and was lying in his blankets under Calloway's wagon, too sick to sit up.

Charley Twigg came to me saying, "You are wanted at Calloway's wagon. Go quickly. I'll hold your baby." I gave him the child and went over to the wagon as directed.

There was the sick man under the wagon, and I observed our ex-captain walking towards us with my husband and talking very excitedly.

Our captain had a revolver in his hand and he was very angry because Mrs. B. had allowed Pritchard to ride. We all felt that he really had the intention of killing Pritchard. He abused Mrs. B. for permitting the man to ride, when he should have been walking, as he said.

I stepped between the angry man and Pritchard and told him that I was the one who had told him that the man had been too sick to walk, and I further said, "Mr. C., you made your own brother walk when he was too sick to do so, and he died, and you ought to be in better business than abusing women." He turned and walked away, and we saw nothing more of the revolver.

We saw in the distance the mountains that we understood we would have to climb. We traveled on by a place called Beckwith's and camped at the foot of the mountain for the night so as to have a fresh, early start the next morning. The old emigrant road was laid out by men who realized that they could not do very much grading, so it was up hill to the top, and downhill on the other side to the bottom, never around the hill.

The first mountain was very steep, and even the women had to get out and walk so as to lighten the load. Mrs. Corbin, my two children and I went on ahead.

It was too hard work to carry both children at the same time, so I carried my baby ahead about a hundred yards and made a sort of cache for her and placed her in it, then I returned and carried my little boy on up the hill a hundred yards beyond the other child and cached him in the same way, and so on up the long, weary mountain.

I had just about gotten my children up to the top when my husband called for me to come back, so leaving the children, I hurried back to the wagon and found that one of our oxen had become balky and was trying to turn around and go back down the mountain.

My husband being alone since the deserters left had more than he could handle. I had never driven oxen, but I had always been used to horses when a girl, and I had petted our oxen a good deal, and I believe they knew me. I went to each of them, patting them and calling them by name.

When I came to the fractious ox and called him by name, I patted him, and then spoke out loud to them, telling them to "get up;" at the same instant I gave old "Star," the fractious ox, three or four smart blows with the ox-whip and away they went up the mountain, and we never had any more trouble.

When descending the mountain, further on, the road was so steep at one place that all of the wagons had to be let down again with ropes, and one wagon tipped over, spilling out supplies all over the mountain side.

Letting Down a Wagon

Some way, though, everything was righted, and we at last reached a place that seemed intended for the habitation of white people and that was American Valley in Plumas County. This was a beautiful little valley resting among the mountains, and its hundreds of acres of level fields were very attractive to us.

My husband's diary shows that we arrived in American Valley September 16, and his notes at this point might be interesting:

Sept. 17 Warm, but cool at night. Laid over today. Here we obtained some fine vegetables at.- potatoes 25 cts., cabbage 20 cts., turnips 10 cts., er pound. This is quite a treat. The north fork of Feather River runs through this valley and is supplied with fine trout, - there is a good business done in this valley, and there are diggings all around it that are paying well - gardening is good business here, also.

We continued on our journey, though our party was much smaller. Our train had been originally eleven wagons, now there were only three, and we ourselves had but five oxen and were using a smaller wagon. Our route was out by a place called Spanish Ranch and thence through Meadow Valley and again up a steep mountain road. My husband's diary gives the following notes at this point:

Sept. 20th. Frost this morning. Got a late start. Passed down a large, beautiful valley of good land to Rich Valley (Buck's Ranch) three miles and over to a ridge to another valley. Here we cut grass for the mountain tomorrow and moved down the valley some four miles at the lower end of the grass and camped; have gone only eight miles today. Hay sells along here at 10 cts. per pound, beef, 25 cts. and 30 cts., pork 45 cts., flour 45 cts., also, and whiskey 25 cts. per "swig."

Sept 21. Warm, but hard frost this morning. Got a good start and took to the hills which are more down than up - road, rough and crooked - and went to Pea Vine Ranch at dusk after a hard day's drive, 18 miles (this road passes down the dividing ridge between North and Middle Feather River, and is called a good mountain road, but is only used for packing out as it is worse going up than coming down - wagons come down this road that cannot go back), and camped - no grass and poor water - this spring is 500 or 600 feet below our camp of last night, and it is much warmer here; we have been rapidly descending since we crossed the summit range on the tenth.

22nd. Got out early and traveled over a rough, cooked and hilly road going down some very steep hills passing a sawmill (poor concern) to camp on the mountains without grass or water. Cut some oak trees and let our cattle browse there.

We soon reached the low lands, or "plains," as they were called in Butte or Yuba county, and proceeded by way of a little settlement called Wyaddotte to Sewell's Ranch, a few miles from Marysville, the county seat of Yuba.

Here our journey as an emigrant train practically ended, and it was here that the remnant of our train disbanded, the individuals of the company going in different direction to the various mining camps. My husband and I remained in this place several days to rest, and to make preparations for a journey to the reported rich placer diggings at Camptonville, Yuba county, some forty miles further north.

We sold all but three oxen and traded our heavier wagon for a lighter one into which we loaded all of our earthly possessions, including some provisions and supplies that we had lately purchased, and after a few days' rest we commenced our lonely journey toward the diggings.

V

GARDEN VALLEY

It was early October that we arrived at a little valley some five or six miles below Camptonville called Garden Valley. Here we determined to remain for the winter, as we were not prepared for the cold and snow that we were advised would be encountered at Camptonville. This little valley was located just below the line of deep snow, and so we felt that it would be better for us not to tempt Providence by taking chances on encountering a hard winter.

We here met an old-time Indiana friend, a Mr. Acheson, who permitted us to occupy a big double log house belonging to him. No sooner was the permission granted than we unloaded our effects and moved into our temporary home and busied ourselves in cleaning house and putting things in order.

We sold our oxen at a fair price, and I bought a fine milk cow, paying therefore the rather princely sum of $425, gold coin. The log house seemed like a palace after six months of dreary travel over desert and sleeping in a small tent or a canvas-covered wagon.

We made ourselves as comfortable as possible, but that is not saying much, as the inside of the building was not sealed with boards, the walls being the sides of the original logs and the spaces between them were not chinked or filled with other smaller timbers or mud, as was the custom, and there were great spaces that we never did fill up with anything. We had an abundance of fresh air; in fact, we could have gotten along just as well with less, but we were under cover, it had the semblance of a house, and it was our "home" for a while anyway, and it seemed delightful.

I sewed a lot of barley sacks together and made what we considered t the time a very nice carpet. This was laid in our combined parlor, sitting room and bedroom - there was only one other room, that was our kitchen. Our carpet, when it was laid, called forth many exclamations from our miner friends who called on us. They had not seen anything quite so luxurious as that in the way of house furnishings for a long time, and we had many a visit from miners from nearby "claims" who came in just to sit around and hear the latest news from the "States."

Our nearest neighbors, with the exception of a few miners here and there, were at Foster's Bar, then a very lively mining camp a few miles distant on the north fork of the Yuba River.

Yuba River 1852

The fall passed away quickly, and the rains and cold weather gave us a taste of what we might expect later on. All supplies were hauled from Marysville up by our camp into the mountains by means of huge freight wagons drawn by eight and ten mule teams, and as the roads were not very good anyway, the storms that now ensued made freighting very difficult and expensive, and in consequence food became very scarce and very high priced. For example, we paid that winter $50 for a 50-pound sack of flour, a dollar a pound for butter, and about the same for sugar. The price of commodities was measured in dollars instead of cents. I purchased early in the fall a dozen hens, paying $3 a piece for them, but I soon got my money back on that investment, for the hens were good layers and the miners in the valley were glad to pay me three dollars a dozen for all the eggs I could spare, and I remember that during the "holidays" that winter, eggs went up to four dollars a dozen.

Our cow proved a veritable gold mine, for she gave five gallons of milk a day, only one gallon of which we could make use of ourselves, and I found a ready sale for the other four gallons at three dollars a gallon. There were many Chinamen and Mexicans working on the "bars" in the creeks, and they were always good customers and would buy all the milk and eggs I could spare, and never objected to the price asked.

My two little children were a constant source of interest and pleasure to the miners who called on us, and many a coin their little chubby hands clasped after some rough miner had picked them up and held them aloft and played with them. No doubt the sight of the children called up many pleasant memories of home and family in the "States" that had been left, perhaps never to be seen again.

We experienced a good deal of annoyance from the Indians who had a regular village not far from us. They were the so-called Digger Indians, much inferior to those we saw on the plains. They prowled about and stole a great many things from us, but the worst feature about them was that they would crawl up to the house at night time and look in at us through the cracks between the logs, and my children and myself were frightened many times by them when we were alone. We improved the situation somewhat by getting a fine big dog who became our protector, and from that time on, the Indians did not bother us, though once in a while I would be at work and on looking up suddenly I would see an Indian's face at a hole in the wall peering in at me, but by the time I could call the dog the Indian had disappeared.

Christmas was on the way. We did not know exactly what we should do for the holidays, but something had to be done. The day before Christmas my husband and I determined to have a real Christmas dinner.

To be sure, we could not expect to have a turkey dinner, for the very good reason that there was no such thing as a turkey to be had. We did not wish to sacrifice any of our hens that had been laying so many "golden eggs," and so we had to resort to another expedient.

My husband shouldered his rifle and set out across the valley on a hunt. He didn't know exactly what he wanted to kill - it was anything that would serve as a substitute for the much-wanted turkey. In an hour or two he returned from the hunt with a fine big jack rabbit he had shot. The problem was solved. We soon had the rabbit dressed and ready for the morrow.

That Christmas eve was rather an unhappy one for us - for me in particular. It was the first Christmas that I had ever spent away from home, relatives and friends, and I felt the changed conditions very keenly.

We had no toys for the children and could not get any, and we could not ask the children to hang up their stockings, for Santa Claus wouldn't have found them if they had done so, and we couldn't bear having the stockings empty the next morning.

We had to content ourselves with the hope that by the next Christmas conditions would be improved. I also found some little comfort in the thought that even if the stockings had been hung up that night, they, perhaps, would have been stolen by the prowling Indians.

Christmas Day was bright, clear and beautiful. Garden Valley had the delightful climate of the California foohill region, and on that particular Christmas Day it seemed a veritable garden spot. I baked the rabbit in the little sheet iron stove that I had brought across the plains, and our table, when "set" with our iron knives and forks, tin plates, cups and spoons, not only had on it a finely browned rabbit done to a turn, but a genuine bread pudding.

This pudding deserves some special mention as it was no ordinary affair, made up as it was of flour worth one dollar a pound, milk three dollars a gallon, butter one dollar a pound, sugar one dollar a pound, and eggs three dollar a dozen. And then the sauce made of some dried Chili peaches, a small sack of which we had bought for $20, and good coffee with plenty of good cream from our $425 cow, completed our menu.

My husband had invited a couple of young men to dine with him, Ben Hugg and Charley DeLong, and my recollection is that our guests did complete justice to the meal. We had a good time.

We talked of dear ones at home and planned for the future. We all enjoyed the reunion very much, we had our friends with us, we had a roof over us, we were enjoying good health, and although we were a long distance from the home and friends we held dear, it was Christmas!

We had received an invitation to attend a grand ball that was to be given at Sam Achison's hotel up at Foster's Bar that Christmas night, but my husband and I could not go on account of the children. I was always glad, though, that we did not go, because of the catastrophe that happened there.

It seems the hotel was a two-storey frame building, the ballroom being in the second storey, and the room immediately thereunder being used as the supper room.

They always had a grand ball supper at midnight in those early days, that was really the feature of the ball. People had gathered there from mining camps far and near, and quite a number of ladies came up from Marysville and from wayside places on the wagon road to Marysville.

The dance had been in progress but a short time, and the long tables below set for the hungry dancers were, no doubt, fairly groaning under their weight of good things to eat when suddenly, there was a fearful crash and then screams - the dancing floor had given way and everybody was precipitated to the supper room right on the top of the tables.

Fortunately, no one was killed, although many were hurt. The dance was over, and the supper spoiled. The beams were not of sufficient strength to stand the strain produced by that great crowd of red-shirted and cowhide-booted miners, dancing quadrilles.

The winter of 1852-53 was a particularly severe one in California, not only by reason of the tremendous floods in the lowlands, but there was much suffering in the mountain regions on account of the scarcity of provisions.

We, however, were fairly comfortable for the winter, owing to our foresight in not going on further in the mountains, but of course, our provisions ran rather low, and we felt the want of many things, but the winter finally passed away, and as soon as the roads became passable in the spring we made one more move and finally arrived at the little town of Camptonville, then a very lively and prosperous mining camp.

VI

CAMPTONVILLE

The story of our journey across the plains ends with our arrival at Camptonville, but perhaps it would not be inappropriate to record a few of the events that transpired in those early days in the mines in this closing chapter.

We found Camptonville to be a very lively little mining center. There were rich placer claims being worked in the creeks all about. Rude cabins had been hastily built on all sides, and a sawmill at the upper part of the town turned out lumber for the "diggings," as well as for the construction later of some very substantial residences and some two-storey hotels.

Camptonville, Yuba County, 1860

Among the people making up the population were many professional men from the East - doctors, lawyers, and young men just out of college who had come West to win their fortunes. There were several physicians practicing their profession and a number of lawyers at once "hung out their shingles," and in addition to having mining interests, practiced their profession at the bar in the justice courts where oftentimes very important matters were adjusted.

My husband at once interested himself in mining and secured some very valuable interests. He took a prominent part in public affairs, and was one of the first to take steps for the establishment of schools in the town. Although he was not a lawyer, he was frequently called upon to appear and prosecute and defend cases in the justice courts and had many a successful hard-fought battle in lawsuits when very able lawyers were opposed to him. Among the lawyers who had come to our town at this time were the "two Belchers," as they were called., William C. and Issac Belcher, who were just out of college and who remained there several years practicing their profession. and who afterward became very eminent in the State as lawyers and jurists.

My husband served several years as a deputy sheriff, and this office was attended by great personal danger, as men in those days did not always have respect for the law, and they were often inclined to take the law in their own hands and disregard legal restrictions and requirements. Many times my husband sat up all night guarding property that he taken possession of officially.

Our little house for several years was the place for safekeeping in this way of much property, and I lived in constant fear of violence, as I was the custodian of property during my husband's absence, when in the diggings or away attending to his official business.

The only weapon I had and which I was prepared to use was a full kettle of boiling water that was always kept ready for use, and one night after my husband had levied an attachment and had taken possession of a lot of valuable personal property, including a considerable amount of money, all of which he had stored in our house, my husband being absent, a man came to the door in the middle of the night and tried to get in, saying he wished to look at some records that my husband had, but I told him he couldn't get in; he tried to force the door, and then I got a big dipper of scalding water and went to the door and told him that I had a kettle of scalding water and that if he attempted to come in I would scald his eyes out. No further attempt was made that night.

My husband was also elected by the miners as District Recorder of mining claims, and this was a very important office which he held for several years. He was also a notary public, and several years after held the office of justice of the peace.

My husband's official position and his natural disposition placed him always among those who believed in law and order, and although there were many times when it seemed that the law was too slow to punish crime, he always counseled to allow the law to take its course, and objected to violence. I will relate the circumstances of one affair that caused some little stir in the early 50's.

There was a half-witted fellow there in town whom the "boys" were wont to tease, and a plan was worked out by some of the practical jokers to have some real exciting fun at his expense. So it was arranged that one of the men, a doctor whose name I have forgotten, should get into an altercation with this simple-minded fellow and provoke a quarrel so that the doctor would have an excuse to challenge him to a duel (the *code duello* was then in vogue), and according to program, the quarrel occurred when there was quite a crowd about, and the poor victim was goaded on to apply some insulting epithet to the doctor, who very promptly challenged the "offender" for a duel. Seconds were appointed and the time, place, and conditions of the fight were soon arranged. It was to be a fight at twenty paces with "navy" revolvers. Of course, all of the men about town were on hand, but my husband refused the invitation to be present, declaring that it was wrong, and that no good would come of it.

The affair was proceeded with, and the principals stood facing each other and were handed their weapons loaded - only with powder. At the word, both fired, and the doctor fell as if pierced by a bullet. Some red ink was spilled on his white shirt front, and it was remarked by the surgeon who was present that the man was mortally wounded. Someone told the "victor" that as he had killed his man he had better get out of town as quickly as he could, as he was liable to be lynched if he didn't. The poor fellow did not wait for a second invitation, but dropped his revolver and ran away as fast as his legs could carry him. To further carry out the joke, some of the men started after the fugitive yelling, and firing their revolvers. The frightened man soon disappeared in the trees at the south of the town, and the incident closed.

Nothing more was heard of the man, and it was supposed that he had gone to some other mining camp, and the matter was forgotten. Some two weeks later, a posse of deputy sheriffs was scouring the country below town looking for the trail of some stage robbers, and one of their number walking along at the bottom of a steep precipice about half a mile from town came across the corpse of a man. It was in an advanced stage of decomposition and was hardly recognizable, but the clothes and certain things found about it proved conclusively that the body was that of the late fugitive from the duel.

The top of the cliff was covered with trees and underbrush, and the poor fellow in his excitement and his desire to get away had rushed over this fatal place and broken his neck. The man's name was never found out, and nothing was ever done by the authorities as the ringleaders suddenly became very close-mouthed about the affair.

Camptonville, as I have stated, was located on the regular stage line running from Marysville on the south to Downieville on the north, and was about forty miles distant from either place. The stage was the only means of shipping out gold dust from the mines up north, and this fact attracted many of the lawless element who seized every opportunity they could to rob the stage of its precious express matter, and there were many such robberies extending over a number of years.

A bold attempt was made to rob the stage some time in 1853 or 1854. There was some $60,000 in gold dust in the express boxes belonging to the "Campbell boys," who were in the stage guarding their treasure.

When the stage arrived in Camptonville there was considerable apprehension felt that an attempt would be made during the journey to Marysville, and several men, including my husband, volunteered to make the trip and help guard the express. I begged my husband not to go, but he was determined, and arming himself joined the expedition. His account of the attempted hold-up was as follows:

We had passed the Oregon House (wayside inn) and the stage with its fourteen passengers, including the express messenger sitting on the outside with the driver, was slowly ascending a grade near "Dry Creek," when I heard someone near the stage call out, "Stop that team and throw up your hands!" I heard the express messenger say to the driver, "Drive on you ---, or I'll blow your head off."

The stage went on and at the same time there ensued a perfect fusillade of pistol shots. The messenger kept up a steady fire with his revolver, answered by shots from the robbers. Most of the passengers were armed and everybody who could poke his revolver out fired away at the retreating robbers. The latter were evidently taken by surprise by the resistance we made and they slowly retreated. I saw the leader sitting on a horse some sixty yards away deliberately firing at us with his navy revolver, and between shots lustily cursing his men for their cowardice, but he failed to rally them.

The old stage was fairly riddled with bullets, and one struck a Negro woman, going through her lungs. She was sitting next to me and fell in my arms. Strange as it may seem, although some thirty bullets struck the stage, the Negro woman was the only one injured.

The captain of the robbers still sat on his horse in plain view, and the messenger resting his revolver on the top of the stage took several shots at him, and we saw him after one shot jerk up the hand that held the bridle, and then he rode away. The stage had never stopped, and we did the best we could for the wounded woman and finished our journey without being further molested.

We soon came up with one of the Campbells, who had ridden ahead on a mule. We found him at the side of the road minus mule and revolvers, the robbers having relieved him of both, and made him walk on ahead. A few months afterward, a desperado was caught in one of the counties south of us. A bullet wound in his left hand, and a bullet hole through the knot of the leather bridle was some evidence of his being the leader of the gang.

A few years later the Civil War commenced, and we found that there were many Southern sympathizers in our community. It was feared that the guerrillas would come across and take the State for the South, and early in the war militia companies were organized throughout the State and one such company was organized in Camptonville called the Yuba Light Infantry.

The existence of the Knights of the Golden Circle made the military company a necessity, and many a night every member of the company took his musket home with him and held himself ready for instant call. A picture of this company was taken on the 4th of July, 1863, while they were out on parade, and it is published here as a relic of the war times.

Yuba Light Infantry on parade, July 4, 1863

Many of the residents of Camptonville immediately on the breaking out of the war left for the East via Panama to take part in the struggle, and I recall one instance of one of these men returning after the war - Billy Gibson, who lived there for many years afterward, and who was only recently an inmate of the Solders' Home at Sawtelle. We were all anxious as to the outcome of the war. It made it all the more uncertain for us because it took a month for news to get to San Francisco. The rebels were organized and armed in our neighborhood, but the pressure of our "home guard" of sixty men kept them at bay.

The great conflict came to an end and then we heard the awful news of the assassination of President Lincoln. The Union people among us were heart-broken, and the rebels jubilant. One rebel, a prominent hotel-keeper, so far forgot himself as to remark in the bar-room of his hotel in the presence of a lot of Union men when the news was received, "The news is too good to be true." The Union men present jumped to their feet and denounced the utterer of those horrible words and steps were taken to hang the offender, and I verily believe that only one thing savef him from being strung up to the nearest tree, and that was the fact that he was a Mason.

The hope we had in our hearts for ultimate success in our venture into the New Eldorado was expressed by the words of a little song that some young fellows fresh from college sang one night as a serenade under our windows:

"Hard times come again no more."

MARY ALEXANDER VARIEL

VII

THE VARIEL FAMILY

Variel House, Plumas County, 1878

   The Variels were among the first emigrants from the East to travel through the American Valley during the Gold Rush. Joshua Variel practiced law in Camptonville in Yuba County until 1878, when he moved the family to Quincy. He and his son William built this house. The Variel family sold the house in 1896 when they moved to Los Angeles.

Joshua And Mary Variel And Family

Florence Variel, Daughter of Joshua and Mary

Joshua Variel And Florence Leaving Quincy For Los Angeles

Joshua Variel And Grandson Alexander

Judge William James Variel
Born in 1861 in Camptonville

Robert and William Variel in their Los Angeles law office

HON. R. H. F. VARIEL

Robert Henry Fauntleroy Variel, was born November 22, 1849, is the oldest of five children born to Joshua and Mary Alexander Variel.

He emigrated from Indiana with his parents in 1852, traveling across the plains by ox-team. The family reached California in September 1852 and spent the winter, one of the hardest in the history of the state to that time, in a log cabin on a branch of the North Fork of the Yuba River. Early in the spring of 1853, the family moved to Camptonville, which was becoming a prosperous gold mining camp in the gravel mines between the North and Middle forks of the Yuba River.

They remained in Yuba County for several years: "The father was a man of excellent habits and character, and of diligent industry, but without business training or the faculty of accumulating wealth, although possessed of a clear and vigorous understanding."

Because Joshua Variel "could not stand the work of mining" he worked instead as a carpenter and millwright. He also served as Justice of the Peace for 12 years and then practices law in the justices' courts for many years afterward.

Robert, the eldest Variel son, showed ability in school and study, and ultimately decided he would go into law as a career as well. Since the frontier schools of the day provided little opportunity in this regard, he was sent away to school; he was away for six months in the winter of 1865-66.

From 1866 to 1868, he made excellent progress in his studies with the instructor A. G. Drake, who taught in the ungraded public school at Camptonville during that time. Robert also studied with the Hon. E. A. Davis, who became a superior judge of Yuba and Sutter counties.

At age 18, Robert applied for the credential that allowed him to teach in the public schools in Yuba County, and he immediately began his career as a teacher and taught in various country districts over the next five years. All the while, he continued his studies and in 1870 obtained a first-grade state certificate, which allowed him to teach at a higher level.

In 1871 he moved to Plumas County and taught in the public school in Crescent Mills, where he remained until 1873, when he was nominated to run for the position of district attorney in Plumas County on the Republican ticket.

He was elected in that "strongly Democratic county" by a considerable majority despite having little formal education in the law. He continued to read law while practicing it at the same time. He was by all accounts successful in his discharge of the office, holding the position for nine years until he voluntarily declined to run again.

He married Caroline Vogel, an educator, in 1876. She was a native of New York who had worked as a hired girl in California in a mining and lumber town and then taught school. They had three children.

After the marriage, Robert was admitted to general practice as an attorney in the district court; in 1879, he was admitted to the state supreme court.

"It may be of some interest to know that Mr. Variel's reading and study of law was at all times pursued entirely alone and without the aid of instructors, and that he first read the Annotated Penal and Political Codes of California, with the California Supreme Court Decisions cited in the notes under the several code sections.

This course of legal study was of his own selection, and was dictated in part by the circumstance that his library, as district attorney, consisted of the California Reports, Statutes and Codes, but mainly by his necessities, as being the uninformed legal adviser of the other county officers, and the untrained public prosecutor of criminals, who had much of that work to do."

Robert Variel was elected on the Republican ticket to the state assembly in 1886, representing Plumas and Sierra counties. He was appointed chairman of its judiciary committee. and also worked on the committees on mining, corporations, constitutional amendments and elections. He was instrumental in passing several important bills, including the Wright irrigation act and the act endowing the State University with permanent support.

During this session of the legislature, "a bitter war was carried on between the advocates of the miners and farmers, growing out of the efforts of the latter to make the dumping of tailings in the mountain streams a felony, and of the former to enact a law, introduced by Mr. Variel in the assembly, providing that the miners might mine and discharge their tailings into the streams, on condition of first putting in restraining dams; and Mr. Variel became the acknowledged leader of the miners' fight in the assembly."

Robert Variel left Plumas in 1887, settling in San Francisco. Due to failing health, he moved to Los Angeles in January of 1888 and began the practice of law there. "Within a few months after coming to Los Angeles a temporary association in the law practice was formed with Hon. Stephen M. White."

As stated in the Historical and Biographical Record of Los Angeles County and Vicinity, "With none of the adventitious aids of fortune or wealth, Mr. Variel, through the observance of good habits and by reason of unremitting perseverance, study, toil and diligence, aided by his capacity to win and retain friends, has achieved a career that may well serve as an example to every ambitious young man who would rise at the bar, but finds himself poor, without education or training, and without influential friends."

From Historical And Biographical Record Of Los Angeles And Vicinity containing a history of the City from its earliest settlement as a Spanish Pueblo to the closing year of the Nineteenth Century by J. M. GUINN , A. M., Secretary of the Historical Society of Southern California. Member of the American Historical Association of Washington, D. C., Chapman Publishing Company, Chicago,1901, pp. 752-754

TRANSCRIPT OF
DEATH NOTICE OF J.H. VARIEL

Joshua Hutchings Variel Died Yesterday At His Residence No. 2215 East Fourth Street In The Eighty-Third Year Of His Age. Mr. Variel Was The Father Of R.H.F. Variel, William J. Variel, Florence M. Variel, Mrs. Mary E. Barstom Of Napa And Mrs. B.C. Eaton Of Ventura. He Was A Member Of Los Angeles Commandery, K.T., And Al Malaskah Temple, Order Mystic Shrine.

From the front page of the Los Angeles Herald, March 4, 1905

Pioneer Woman Passes Away

Mrs. Mary Variel, One of the Early Settlers, Dies at Her Home at the Age of Eighty-one Years

Mrs. Mary Alexander C. Variel, widow of the late J.H. Variel, passed away at her resdient 2215 East Fourth Street, Boyle Heights, yesterday. She was 81 years of age.

Mrs. Variel came to Los Angeles with her husband in 1893, the couple having up to that time and since 1892? resided in the northern part of the state.

Their sons, R.H. F. and William J. Variel, well known members of the local bar, had come to Los Angeles several years before, and their parents wished to spend their last days near their boys.

Mr. and Mrs. Variel were pioneers of this state, having crossed the plains by ox team in 1852, and settling, as did most of the eastern flood then pouring into the west, to the mining regions in the north. Their first permanent home was in the town of Camptonville, and here were formed associations and friendships with many whose names subsequently became familiar in California history, including Judges I.H. and William S. Belcher, N.D. Rideout, Stephen J. Field, Judge E.A. Davis, and many others.

Mrs. Variel was born in Stewartsville, Posey County, Ind., February 19, 1827, being the daughter of James Casey and Nancy Downey, members of well known families in the then far west. She was married to Joshua H. Variel, a native of

Maine, in 1848 at New Harmony, Ind. where shere born to them their two first children, Robert and Rose, the latter the wife of Edward Eaton of Ventura.

The early days of the young couple in California were marked by the stirring actions, remarkable events and privations so well known to the pioneer, and in this state were born to them their son, William J. Variel, Mary, now the wife of H.M. Barrow of Los Angeles, and Miss Florience M. Variel, all of whom with their sister Nelle, survive the mother. Mrs. Variel was a general favorite with her acquaintances, a steadfast friend and good neighbor. A mother in Israel, even in her early years she was a favorite and "mothered" many of the young men, who found themselves in this new world, far from all home belongings. It was her great delight to recall and give to her friends the story of pioneer days, and her sons have added to California history by transcribing for print the tales from their mother's life.

Transcript Of The Obituary Of Mary Alexander Variel, Los Angeles Herald, 20 Apr 1907; Page 12

VIII

MAPS

1. New Harmony to Evansville

2. Cairo to St. Louis to St. Joseph

3. St Joseph to the Ferry

4. North and South Platte Rivers

5. Ferry to Ash Hollow

6. Susan Hale Grave

7. Fort Kearney to Fort Laramie

8. Parting of the Ways to Humboldt Sink

9. Truckee Route from the Humboldt Sink

10. Beckwourth Trail

New Harmoney to Evansville

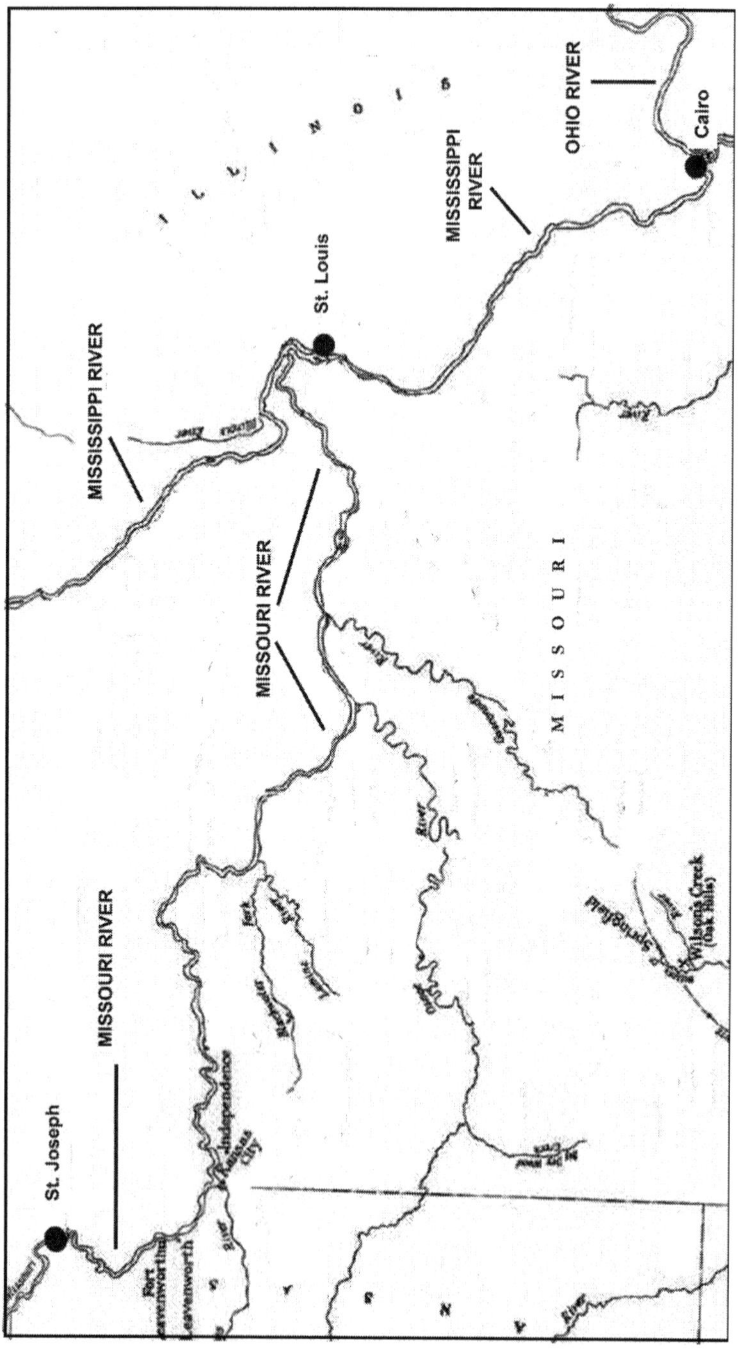
St. Joseph
MISSOURI RIVER
Fort Leavenworth
Leavenworth
Independence
Kansas City
MISSOURI RIVER
MISSISSIPPI RIVER
St. Louis
ILLINOIS
MISSISSIPPI RIVER
OHIO RIVER
Cairo
MISSOURI
Springfield
Wilsons Creek (Oak Hills)

CROSSING THE PLAINS

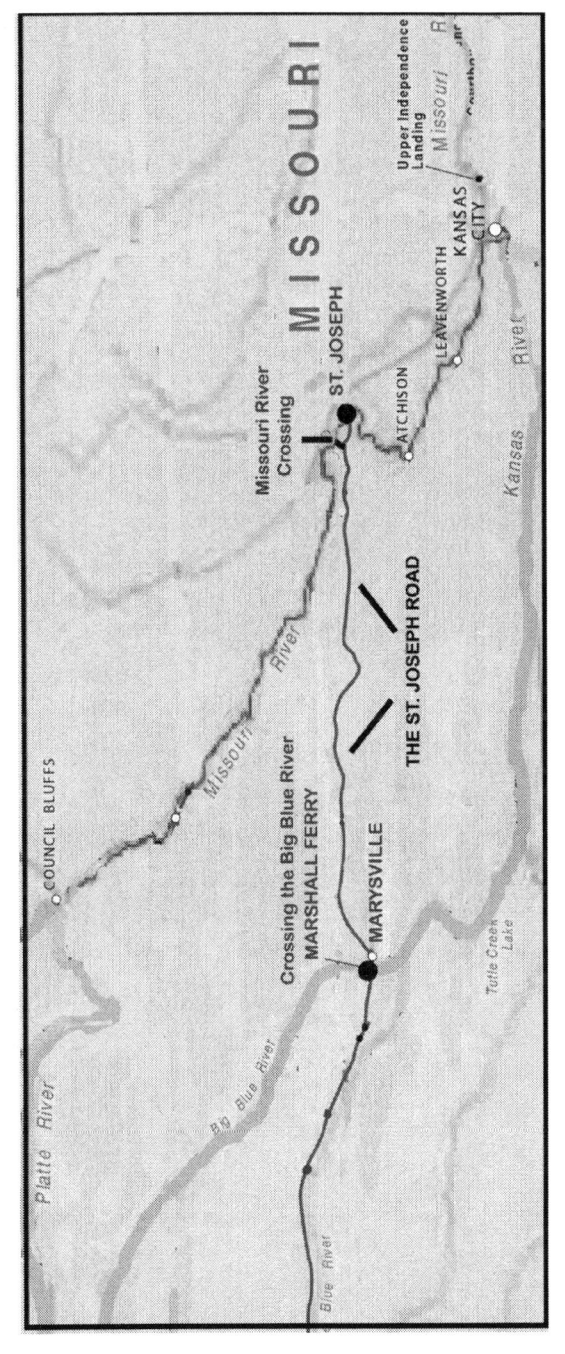

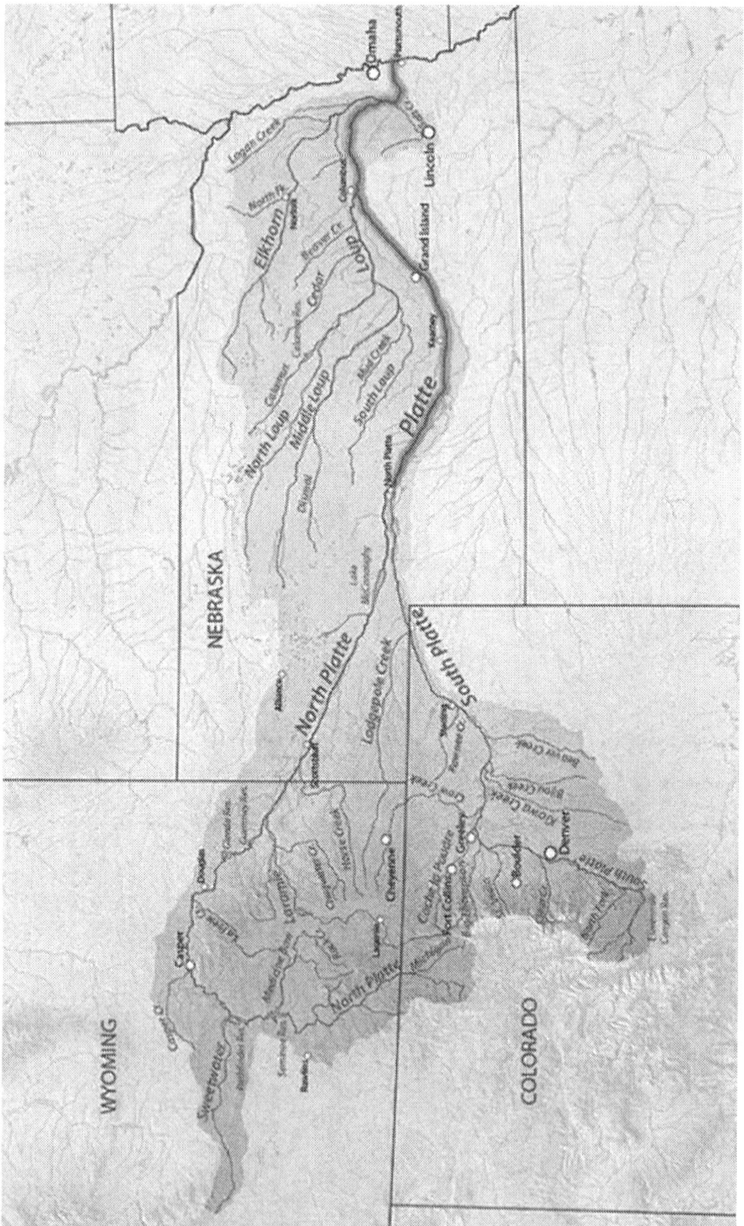
NEBRASKA
WYOMING
COLORADO
Platte
North Platte
South Platte
Elkhorn
Loup
North Loup
Middle Loup
South Loup
Cedar
Lodgepole Creek
Laramie
Sweetwater
Omaha
Lincoln
Grand Island
Denver
Casper
Cheyenne
Fort Collins
Boulder

CROSSING THE PLAINS

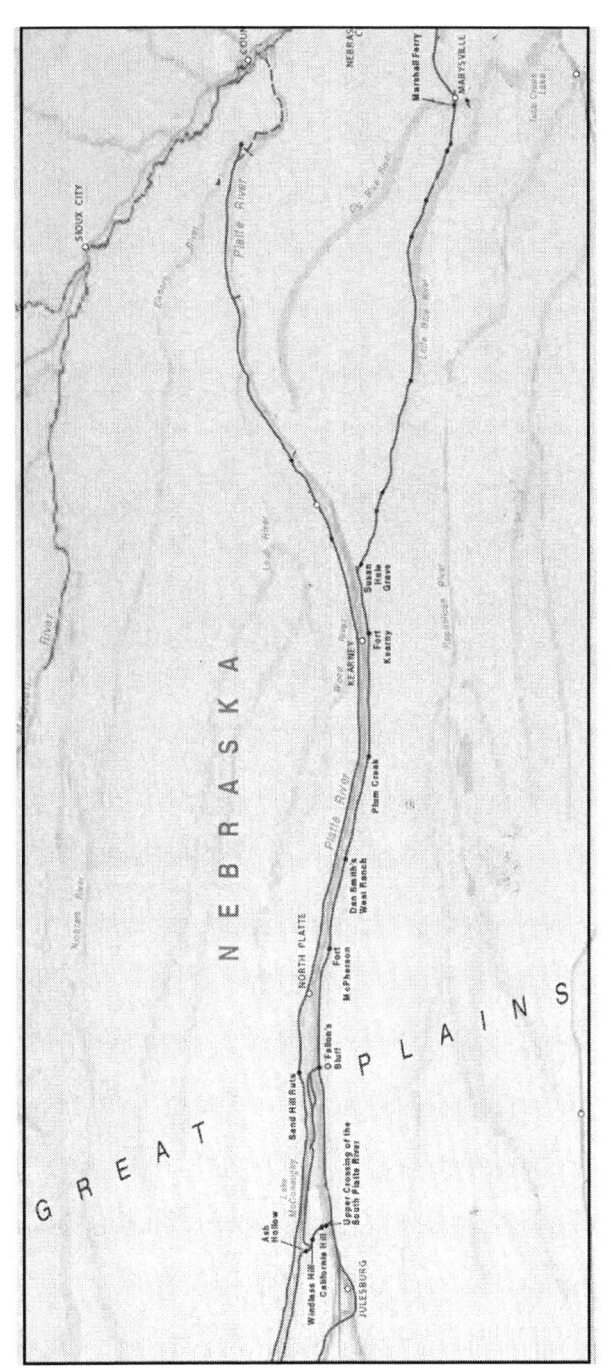

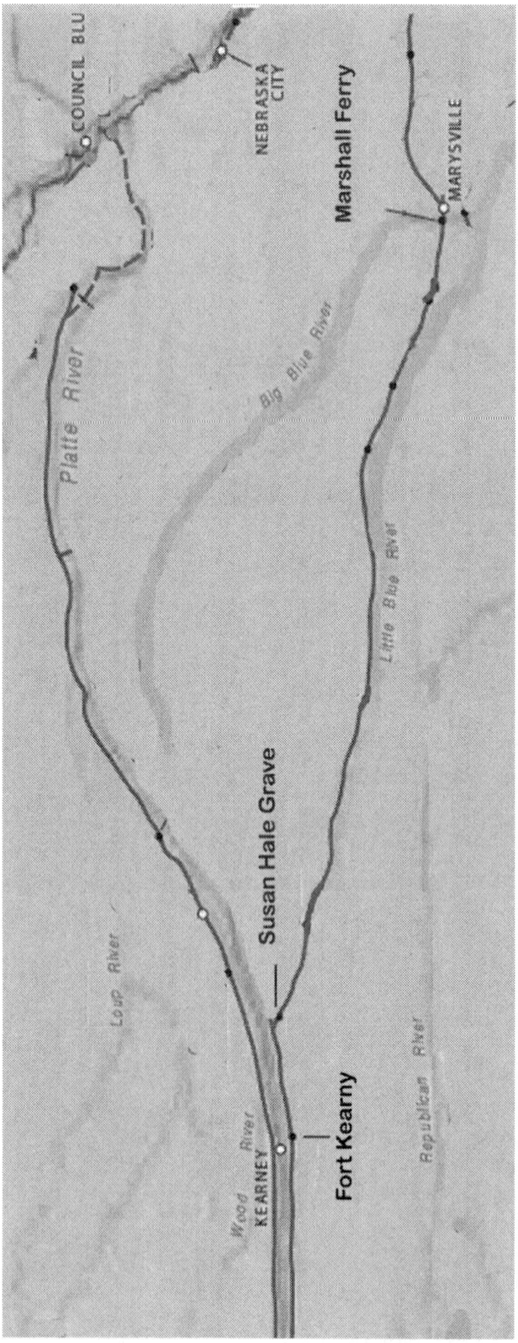
COUNCIL BLU
NEBRASKA CITY
Marshall Ferry
MARYSVILLE
Platte River
Big Blue River
Little Blue River
Susan Hale Grave
Loup River
Republican River
Wood River
KEARNEY
Fort Kearny

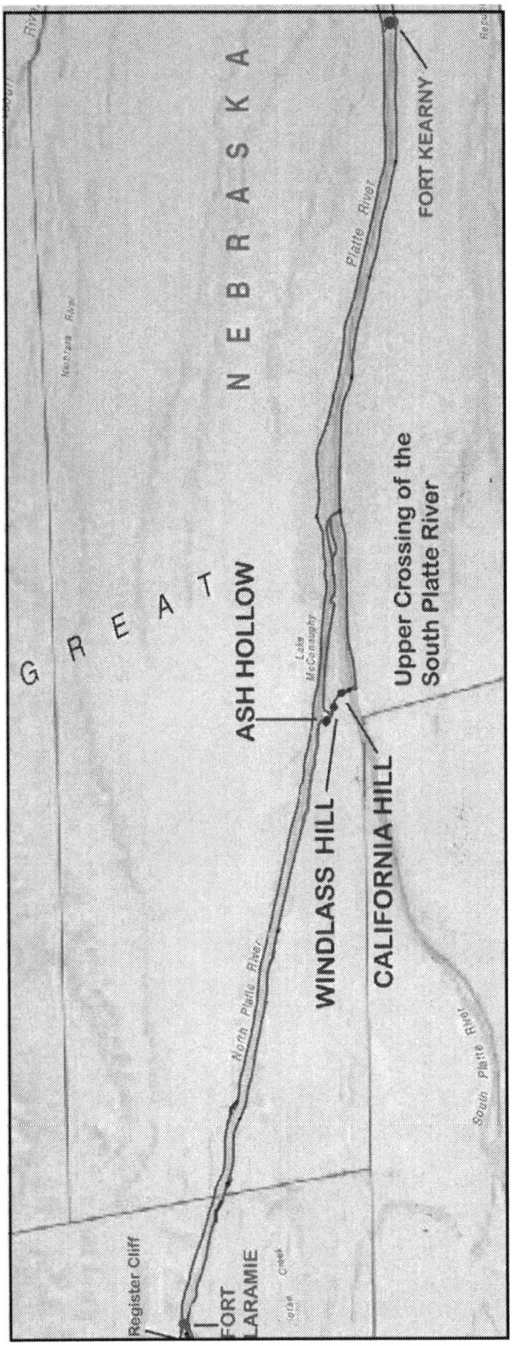

Fort Kearny to Fort Laramie

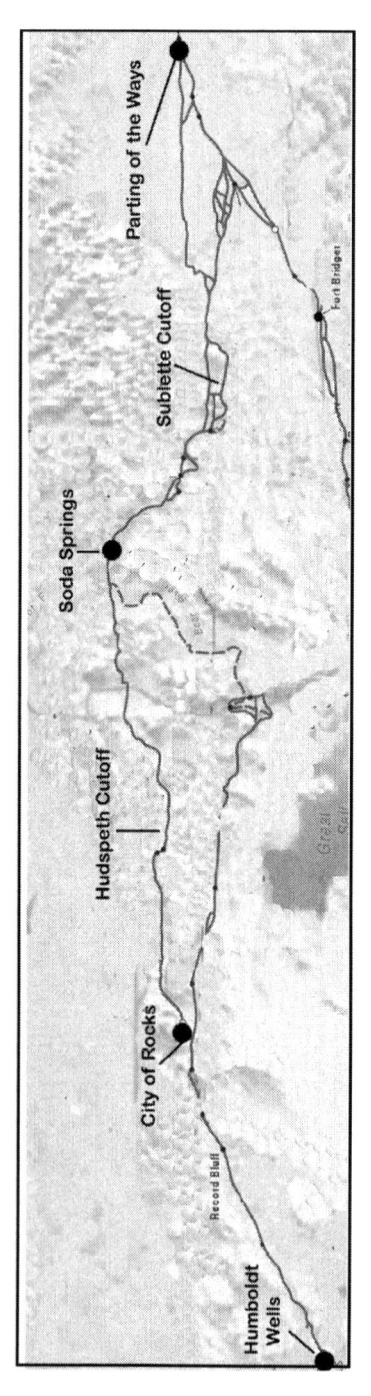

Parting of the Ways to Humboldt Wells

CROSSING THE PLAINS

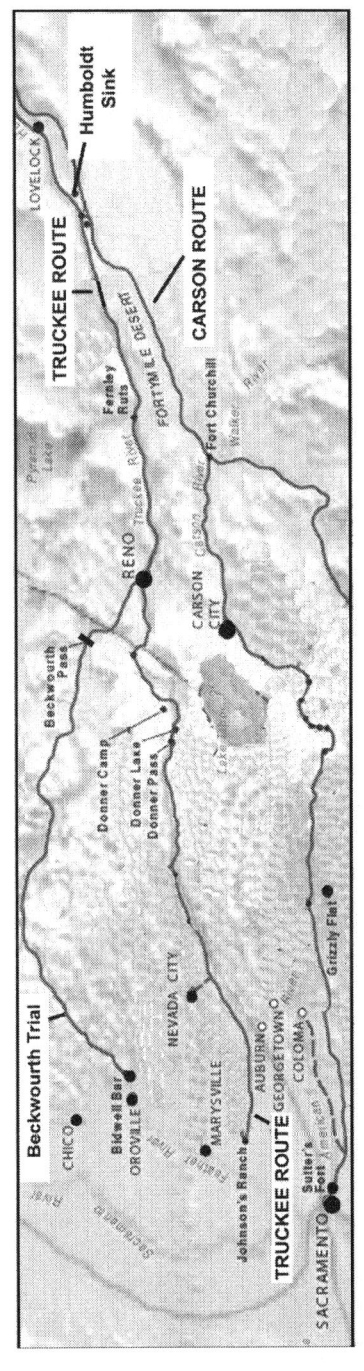

The Truckee Route from the Humboldt Sink

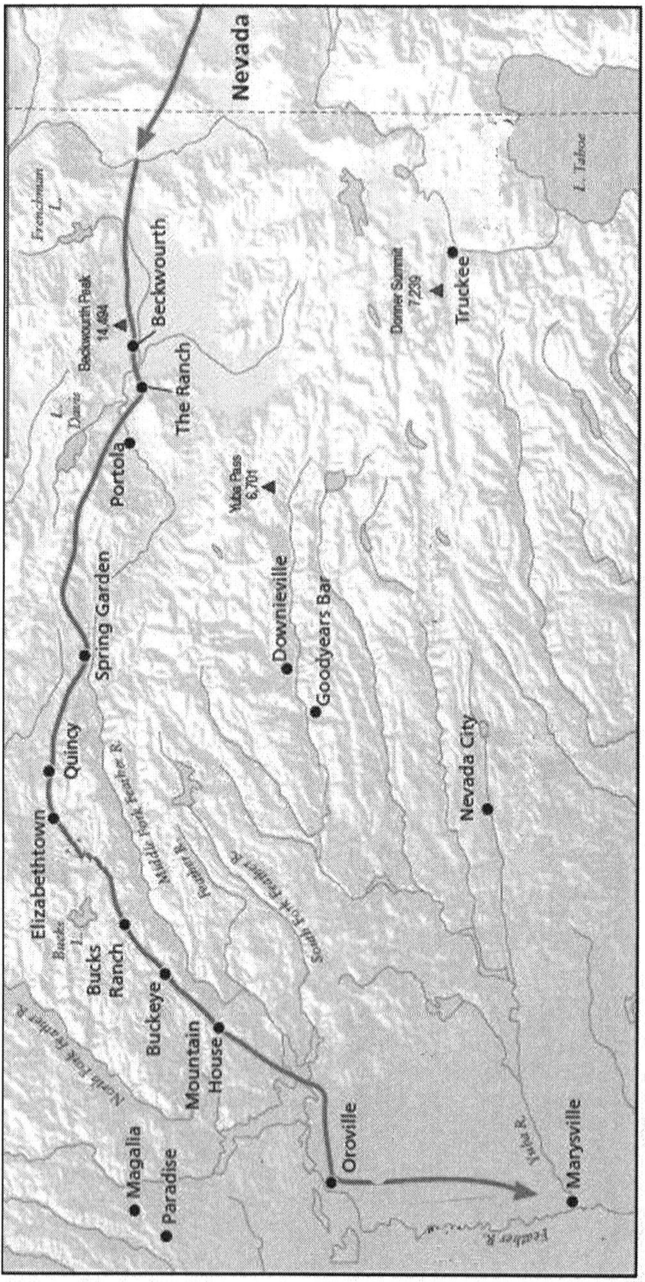

The Beckwourth Trail

IX

NOTES

New Harmony, Indiana
The Variels began their journey from their home in New Harmony, Indiana. It is located on the Wabash River in Posey County. It was established by the Harmony Society in 1814 and purchased by social reformer Robert Owen in 1825 in an attempt to create a utopian community. Although Owen's social experiment was a failure economically, the community became recognized for its advanced education and scientific research. Residents in New Harmony established the first free library and a public school system that was open to both men and women.

New Harmony, Indiana, website, http://www.newharmony-in.gov

Evansville, Indiana
The Variels traveled to Evansville, Indiana, to board a steamboat bound for St. Joseph, Missouri. The city is located on the Ohio River. It was settled by immigrants and the its land was purchased by Hugh McGary Jr., in 1812 and named for Colonel Bob Evans (1783-1844), who fought in the War of 1812 The town was a major commercial center, thriving on the river trade. The construction of the Wabash and Erie Canal, which linked the Ohio River to the Great Lakes, contributed to the city's growth.

http://en.wikipedia.org/wiki/Evansville_indiana

Ohio River
The westward flow of the Ohio River made it a convenient way for pioneer emigrants to move west. After traveling to the mouth of the Ohio River, emigrants like the Variels would go north via the Mississippi River to St. Louis and St. Joseph, Missouri; from either city, they would contuse traveling on the Missouri River or the Mississippi River in their westward migration.

Mississippi River
The Mississippi River is the chief river of the largest drainage system in North America.[3][4] Flowing entirely in the United States (though its drainage basin reaches into Canada), it rises in northern Minnesota and meanders slowly southwards for 2,530 miles (4,070 km)[5] to the

Mississippi River Delta at the Gulf of Mexico. With its many tributaries, the Mississippi's watershed drains all or parts of 31 US states and 2 Canadian provinces between the Rocky and Appalachian Mountains. The Mississippi ranks as the fourth longest and tenth largest river in the world.

Missouri River

The Missouri River is the longest river in North America, Its sources is in the Rocky Mountains of western Montana, and the river flows to the east and to the south for a distance of 2,341 miles before joining with the Mississippi River north of St. Louis, Missouri. The river's drainage takes in over 500,000 square miles, including portions of ten states and two provinces of Canada. The Missouri was a main route to the West in the 19th century.

St. Louis

St. Louis, Missouri, was settled by Native American mound builders who lived in the area from 800 to 1400. In the late 1600s, French explorers came to the region and established a settlement after the French and Indian War in 1764. Its growth resulted from its location as a trading post on the Mississippi River. In 1803, the city and environs were sold to the United States as part of the Louisiana Purchase. In the 1840s, St. Louis became the center of trade with the American West and a major starting point for the western migration.

St. Louis Levee

During the 1840s and 1850s, steamers would often land two or three tiers deep at the levees in St. Louis, Missouri. As historian and Missouri Historical Society director Charles Van Ravensway described the scene at the levee:

> *"St. Louis was still the "River Queen", the greatest inland port in America. As many as 170 gingerbread-trimmed boats jostled one another each day along its six-mile wharf that was lined with untidy stacks of freight and produce. The bustle of the levee was the pride of every true Louisan. The sound of steamship bells and whistles mingled with the noise of tambourine girls, organ grinders, and bagpipe performers, the rasping of the fiddlers, and the musical cries of the apple girls, cigar vendors, and bootblacks. Loafers, drunkards, pickpockets, confidence men, and rowdies from nearby saloons continued to give the area a wicked glitter. Hoards of homeless children darted about, living on their wits and seeking shelter in forgotten corners. Young girls earned a few pennies by exposing themselves to the steamboatmen. Draymen cursed their heavily laden wagons all the way to the landing stages; drivers and carriages and hacks picked their way skillfully through the crowds to deliver or pick up passengers."*

St. Louis: An Informal History Of The City And Its People 1764-1865, Part IV, Chapter 20, Pp. 412-413, by Charles Van Ravensway, edited by Candace O'Connor, Missouri Historical Society

St Joseph

St. Joseph, Missouri, or "St. Joe," was incorporated in 1843. It was a last supply point and starting point on the Missouri River for western pioneers headed for the Oregon territory and the California Gold Rush in the mid-1800s. It was the westernmost point in the United States that could be reached by train until after the American Civil War.

Covered Wagon

Gold Rush pioneers rarely used the large Conestoga wagon as it was considered unwieldy. They needed a wagon that would last several months through very hard travel conditions. Many emigrants used the sturdy, steel-axled Studebaker wagon to carry all their possessions. Small farm wagons were used in the 1840s. These were quite advanced, having complicated undercarriages centered on a kingpin that allowed the front wheels to pivot and make the wagon turn easily. The front wheels of these wagons were smaller than the back wheels, which also helped make sharp turns on the trail. The wagons typically had cloth covers closed at both ends to keep out the ever-present dust. The covers were treated with linseed oil in hopes of keeping out the rain, but most tended to leak anyway.

Studebaker History
http://www.studebakerhistory.com/dnn/Timeline/tabid/65/Default.aspx (downloaded)

Oxen

When it came to selecting the best way to travel west, most people chose a covered wagon drawn by oxen. Between 50 percent and 75 percent of the emigrants chose oxen to haul their goods. While mules were sometimes used because they were faster, they were also hard to handle. Oxen traveled at a slower pace, but they were tougher and more reliable than mules. Oxen are very strong and were able to drag a fully-loaded wagon up a steep hill, out of a ravine, or extract a wagon from a mudhole. They were also able to live on poor grass along the trail. A large wagon generally needed at least three pair of oxen to pull it; the Variels had four yoke, or eight oxen, pulling their wagon. A yoke of oxen cost between $25 and $68 in the latter part of the 1840s.

Oregon Trail Center
http://www.oregontrailcenter.org/HistoricalTrails/MulesOrOxen.htm

Ferry across the Big Blue River (Marshall)
The Big Blue River is located in Hamilton County, Kansas, near the Platte River. One of its first mentions is in an account of an expedition of 1819 that visited a Kaw Indian village. The river is called the Big Blue to differentiate it from the Little Blue River, which also rises in Marshall County and joins the Big Blue. The Big Blue flows through seven Nebraska counties and of its 285 mile-long course, 100 miles are in Nebraska. The first ferry on the Big Blue was located above the river mouth at Manhattan.

> Root, George A., "Ferries in Kansas, Part III, Blue River," *Kansas Historical Quarterly*, May 1934 (Vol. 3, No. 2), pages 115 to 144, http://www.kshs.org/p/kansas-historical-quarterly-ferries-in-kansas-part-iii-blue-river/17900

Fort Kearny
In 1844, the U.S. Secretary of War recommended that a chain of forts be built along the Oregon Trail from the Missouri River to the Rocky Mountains to protect the western emigrants from Indian attacks. Col. Stephen Watts Kearny, charged with building a new fort, selected a site on Table Creek to be named Fort Kearny.

> J. Goldsborough Bruff recorded his impressions on June 17, 1849, "I visited the Fort . . . This place is as yet merely the site of an intended fort; it has some adobe embankments, quarters of adobe & frame, and a number of tents & sheds. Is on the bank of the Platte, where Grand Island makes a narrow branch of the river between it and the shore."
>
> Quoted at National Park Service, Oregon National Historic Trail, http://www.nps.gov/oreg/planyourvisit/site4.htm

The geographic location of this first Fort Kearny proved to be a mistake. The Table Creek site was not on the main overland trail route, and few emigrants passed it. So the War Department ordered another military station to be built about 200 miles further west on the south bank of the Platte River, halfway between Fort Leavenworth, Kansas, and Fort Laramie, Wyoming. The second Fort Kearny was built in 1848 where many western trails converged. Its buildings surrounded a square parade ground of four acres. A flagstaff was raised in the center, and cottonwood trees were planted around the parade area. It was the only fort between the Missouri River and the Rocky Mountains, and although it was built to as protection from Indian attacks, the fort never experienced a direct attack, and no major Indian fights occurred within its immediate vicinity. Thousands of emigrant wagons camped at the fort every summer, and on some days, more than 500 ox teams passed the outpost. The fort also functioned as an ammunition depot. After the Transcontinental Railroad was completed in 1869, Fort Kearny became less important, and it was discontinued as a military post in 1871. The city of Kearney, Nebraska, was named after the fort, but a postal error put an extra "e" in the name, and this mistake has never been corrected.

Nebraska State Historical Society, NSHS, RG2102:1-7, Fort Kearny, NebraskaStudies.org.
http://www.nebraskastudies.org/0400/frameset_reset.html?http://www.nebraskastudies.org/0400/stories/0401_0135.html; The Robinson Library, http://robinsonlibrary.com/america/uslocal/

The Lone Grave

It has been called "The Lone Grave," and it lies on a sandy knoll about four miles northwest of Kenesaw, Nebraska. Most assuredly, however, when Susan C. Hale died in 1852 hers was not a lone grave. This was in the midst of the "cholera corridor," the segment of Oregon-California Trail between the jumping-off towns on the Missouri River and central Nebraska where thousands of emigrants lie buried, victims of the scourge of overland travel, Asiatic cholera. During the trail era, the grave's location was at the northwestern edge of the dry run over the divide between the valley of the Little Blue and the Platte river. There are probably a hundred other lost graves of emigrants not far from that of Susan Haile, but hers is the only one in the Ft. Kearny area to survive with its identity intact. 1852 was a particularly bad year for cholera, a bacterial disease which struck the digestive system so quickly that one could be "healthy in the morning and dead by nightfall." The sheer number of deaths, especially from contaminated water, helps account for the graves that survive elsewhere from that year's emigration. Wyoming has several: Henry Hill, Mary Homsley, Elva Ingram, Mily Irwin, Quintina Snodderly, William H. Bedford, and Nancy Hill, all originally marked by stone grave markers. Nebraska has the grave of Rachel Winters near Scottsbluff. But the Haile grave is conspicuous by being the only grave of 1852 that can still be identified in the cholera corridor of Nebraska.

Adams County Nebraska Historical Society
http://www.adamshistory.org/index.php?Itemid=42&id=39&option=com_content&task=view

California Hill

California Hill, located near North Platte, Nebraska, where the Platte River splits into two major forks. The South Platte runs in a generally southwest direction towards Denver, while the North Platte runs northeast towards Fort Laramie. All emigrants had to cross the South Platte at some point to get to the North Platte and on towards South Pass. Emigrants used one of several crossings, but the Upper Crossing was most important, since it led directly to Ash Hollow and the best approach to the North Platte. California Hill was the first major grade encountered by emigrants after crossing the South Platte. The pioneers and their wagons had to climb 240 feet over about 15 miles to reach a plateau between the North and South Platte Rivers.

<u>California Hill/Upper Crossing of the South Platte River - Brule, Nebraska,</u>
<u>Jim Riehl, National Park Service, Oregon National Historic Trail,</u>
<u>http://www.nps.gov/oreg/planyourvisit/site5.htm</u>

Ash Hollow / Windlass Hill

Located new present-day Lewellen, Nebraska. After climbing California Hill, pioneers traveled 18 miles across the high plateau between the South and North Platte to descend the 25-degree slope of Windlass Hill into the North Platte Valley via Ash Hollow. Ash Hollow was a favorite stopping place for emigrants as it had ample wood, good water, and grass for their oxen and other stock. At one time, a "soddy" (sod house) existed at the end of the hill and was used by pioneers as a "post office." They would leave their letters for family "back East" and money for postage at the soddy, hoping that an eastbound traveler would take them. Pioneer Howard Stansbury described his travel through Ash Hollow in July of 1852 as follows:

"Here we were obliged, from the steepness of the road, to let the wagons down by ropes...The bottom of Ash Creek is tolerably well wooded, principally with ash and some dwarf cedars...traces of the great tide of emigration...plainly visible in remains of camp fires, in blazed trees covered with innumerable names... total absence of all herbage."

<u>Ash Hollow Complex/Windlass Hill - Lewellen, Nebraska, U.S. National Park</u>
<u>Service</u>
<u>http://www.nps.gov/cali/planyourvisit/site1.htm</u>

Fort Laramie

Fort Laramie was the last stopping place for many pioneers before reaching the Rocky Mountains. Emigrants often lightened their loads before attempting the ascent. John D. Lee left Salt Lake City for California in 1849 and described the condition of the California Trail as follows:

"The road was so lined with wagons...That one would be scarcely ever out of sight of some train. Dust very disagreeable, but not to compare with the stench from dead carcasses which lie along the road, having died from fatigue and hunger. Destruction of property along the road was beyond description, consisting of wagons, harness, tools of every description, provisions, clothing, stoves, cooking vessels, powder, lead, and almost everything, etc. that could be mentioned."

Pioneers crossed the Laramie River west of the fort. The trail became rougher due to the hills and ravines created by the many streams feeding into the North Platte. A positive effect of the swift-flowing waters west of Fort Laramie was the much reduce risk of contracting cholera. Fatal attacks of the disease fell dramatically after leaving Fort Laramie.

Ward, Geoffrey C. and Dayton Duncan,
The West: An Illustrated History. Little, Brown, Boston, 1996, p. 129

Soda Springs
Pioneers on the trail to Oregon and California welcomed the sight of Soda Springs. Here, waters that contained iron and carbon dioxide bubbled up from the earth in fields of hollow cones. Travelers frequently made mention of the phenomenon in their diaries and enjoyed the soda waters, just as Mary Variel wrote in her trip diary. While the cone fields of soda no longer exist, there are still several springs filled with the soda water.

National Oregon/California Trail Center, Montepelier, Idaho,
http://www.oregontrailcenter.org/HistoricalTrails/LocalTrailLandmarks.htm

Register Rock / Register Cliff
Travelers on the California Trail left signs of their passage by inscribing names and dates on several large stone formations along the way. Register Cliff is a large chalk-like outcropping rising about 100 feet above the North Platte River Valley. It was sometimes called Register Rock and thousands of pioneers inscribed their names while traveling along the Oregon, California and Mormon Trails. Some 500,000 emigrants used the trails between 1843 and 1869, Register Cliff is the easternmost of the three prominent emigrant "recording areas" located within Wyoming, the other two being Independence Rock and Names Hill. One of the first inscriptions on the rock was in 1829. Register Cliff was the first camp west after leaving Fort Laramie and the pioneers often rested here for a day or two.

Legends of America website
http://www.legendsofamerica.com/wy-registercliff.html

"Emigrant diaries mention several prominent landmarks beyond Fort Laramie. One was Register Cliff, a soft sandstone formation that served as a message board for the emigrants. The abundance of grass next to Independence Rock made it a welcome stopping point for every train. The goal was to arrive here by the 4th of July to be sure of beating the winter snows to Oregon. Independence Rock is a large, low granite mass resembling a giant turtle and covering about five acres of prairie. It is the most often noted landmark west of Fort Laramie. Emigrants found many fur trappers' names already drawn on the rock and added their own names. Axle grease made of pine tar and hog fat was used to paint some names, and a handful are still visible in sheltered nooks and crannies. Some emigrants carved their names, dates, or initials, but this was much harder work than doing so

in the sandstone of Register Cliff. The Mormons, in one of their many entrepreneurial ventures, had men who would inscribe names for up to five dollars each. In 1860 Sir Richard Burton calculated that there were between forty and fifty thousand names written in one way or another on Independence Rock."

Oregon Trail Mileposts: Obstacles, Landmarks And Cutoff Sites On The Wagon Trail.
Oregon-California Trails Organization
http://www.octa-trails.org/learn/people_places/articles_ot_mile_posts.php

Humboldt River
This river runs through the northern part of Nevada. It is the third longest river in the U.S. at 330 miles. The river does not flow into the ocean, but empties into the Humboldt Sink and offers the only natural route for transportation across the Great Basin.

40 Mile Desert
A large barren stretch of alkali wasteland without water. It now known as Nevada's Lahontan Valley. For emigrants to California, this was the most dreaded portion of the journey. Pioneers usually traveled at night across this wilderness to take advantage of the cooler temperatures. The desert was first crossed in 1843 with the first wagon train. Although it was a terrible experience, it became the accepted pathway to California as it split into two main trails: Carson River and Truckee River routes. The route presented the danger of starvation for both humans and animals. In 1850, 1,061 dead mules, nearly 5,000 horses, over 3,700 cattle, and 953 graves were found along the trail. The route was most heavily used between 1849 and 1869.

Nevada Landmarks
http://www.nevada-landmarks.com/ch/HM26.htm

Beckwourth Pass
This is the lowest mountain pass in the Sierra Nevada range with an elevation of 5,221 feet. It is located 20 miles east of Portola, California, and 25 miles northwest of Reno, Nevada. The pass was discovered in 1850 by James Beckwourth, who traveled from Truckee Meadows (Sparks, Nevada) into California and on to Marysville. He led the first wagon train through the pass in 1851. It is estimated that 1,200 emigrants used this route between 1851 and 1854. It was used until about 1855 when the railroads replaced wagon trains as the most favored method for getting to California.

The Beckwourth Trail
http://www.beckwourth.org/Trail/

Elizabethtown

A town along the Beckwourth Pass frequented by pioneers traveling to California during the Gold Rush. It was initially called Tate's Ravine for Alex and Frank Tate who found gold there. In 1852, the town housed between 10 and 15 families; by 1856, it had 2,500 residents who were looking for gold in the area and more than 50 businesses. At its peak, the town boasted 200 members of the Sons of Temperance Society. The name was changed to honor the only unmarried woman in the town, Elizabeth Stork Blakesley.

Sierra Nevada Geotourism Map Guide
Elizabethtown (No. 231 California Historical Landmark)
http://www.sierranevadageotourism.org/content/elizabethtown-no-231-california-historical-landmark/sie6B3E752AC896E2209

Spanish Ranch

In July of 1850, two Spanish men established a camp in Meadow Valley just north of Old Oroville-Quincy Road, six miles west of Quincy, California, where they raised cattle for beef. The area was known as Spanish Ranch and became a distribution hub for the surrounding mining camps. By 1852, the town had grown substantially and featured a hotel, blacksmith shop and general store. In 1868, Wells Fargo opened an office there.

California State Parks - Office of Historic Preservation
California Historical Landmarks Program
http://ohp.parks.ca.gov/

Buck's Ranch

Near Spanish Ranch, the area was rich in gold, silver and copper and became an important mail and stage stop during the Gold Rush. Travelers paid a toll on the Old Stage Road between Quincy and Oroville. The ranch was settled by Horace Bucklin and Francis Walker, Bucklin being its namesake. The buildings of the ranch were destroyed by fire and then flooded by Buck's Lake when a dam was built in 1925.

California State Parks - Office of Historic Preservation
California Historical Landmarks Program
http://ohp.parks.ca.gov/

Foster's Bar

Names for William M. Foster, a miner and merchant who opened a store on the west bank of the North Yuba River in 1849 between Willow and Mill Creeks. In 1850, Blake and Taylor opened a meat market there, and the town quickly became one of the most populous in the area. A post office was also established in 1850 and the town became a voting precinct for all citizens in the region. Population in 1850 has been estimated at between 500 and 1,200. There were several hotels, five stores, numerous saloons, gambling houses, butcher shops, blacksmith shops, and other commercial entities. The top hotel was the El Dorado, owned by the Atchison Brothers, who had a ranch in Slate Range Township and sold milk to the miners.

"A toll bridge was constructed across the river in the fall of 1850, by E.S. Gifford & Company. Gifford was a Quaker, and was killed by Indians in 1852. The bridge was carried away in the winter of 1850-1 by high water. It was rebuilt the next summer and again carried away that winter. James Stewart had an iron boat at this point that he used for ferrying purposes. Atchison & Rice constructed the bridge called Foster Bar bridge in 1854. The flood of 1862 raised the river fifteen feet, carried off Batchelder's store, and did other damage. The river bed was filled up from fifteen to eighteen feet with tailings from the mines. In 1851, the town began to decline. The population was reduced to two hundred and fifty, and the number of stores to three,"

Chapter Xxxi, Foster Bar Township, <u>History Of Yuba County California</u>, Thompson & West, 1879, With Illustrations

Yuba Light Infantry

The Yuba Light Infantry had its roots in a Union League Club organized in 1863. This was formed to counteract the Knights of the Golden Circle, a pro-slavery secret society, which was said to exist in the county at the time. Company E, First Battalion, Fourth Brigade N. G. C. was organized in Camptonville on November 7, 1863, with eighty members. The first officers were: J.P. Brown, Captain; J. G. McClellan, First Lieutenant; S. W. Wardner, Second Lieutenant; Charles Fray, Junior Second Lieutenant. The company was supplied with regulation Springfield breech-loading muskets. The company held regular drills on the second Saturday evening of each month. The company rented a building in 1863 to be used as an armory, although it had been originally constructed as a shingle factory by O. P. Brown. In 1864, the company bought it for $450, which had been raised by subscription by its members. Also in 1864, the building was enlarged and used both as an armory and a dancing hall. A new armory was built in 1877, comprising a space 26 ft. by 92 ft., and two grand balls were given by the military in this hall. In the spring of 1877, rhe "Wilbur & Mills' Minstrel Troupe"was the first group to use the stage. The Yuba Light Infantry organized a 9-piece military band in 1878 called the Camptonville Brass Band. The company purchased the instruments and the musicians enlisted, then formed the band. The company had a target range on the bedrock near the town.

"During the Civil War, two large and well-drilled companies were maintained in the city (Marysville). These not only were of value at home as a safeguard against disorder, but also furnished from their ranks a great many disciplined soldiers to fight for the old flag in the field. A pioneer recalls that during the Civil War the mountains of Yuba County provided a military company. It was at the Oregon House that this command always rallied. They were called the Yuba Mountaineers. Browns Valley, Camptonville and Bullard's Bar also had military organizations about this time. These were known as the Hooker Guards, the Bullard's Guards, and the Yuba Light Infantry."

History of Yuba County California, Thompson & West, 1879, With Illustrations

---

A description of the pioneer travelers as written in the Saint Joseph (Missouri) Gazette newspaper, Wednesday, May 5, 1852:

SAINT JOSEPH GAZETTE

California Emigrants.

There never has been in the history of St. Louis a time when they were so many strangers in our city. In nearly every street, and at the turn of nearly every corner, you see men and women preparing to cross the Plains. The emigration will be larger this than during any preceeding year. At least this is our opinion, for the numbers we see in our streets, and the crowds that arrive on every boat. Boats from the Ohio, Illinois and other rivers, come in crowded to excess, and every boat for the Missouri has more than she can accommodate.

A marked feature of the emigration this year is the number of women who are going out by the land route. Heretofore, the emigrantion by this way has been mostly men, but now a large proportion are ladies and children. We see and hear of a large number of families going, come in companies and other singly or in small parties. With proper provisions and traveling conveniences, it is a trip which a lady may make with pleasure, and benefit to her health.

Notwithstanding the experience of many who have heretofore travelled this route, there seems to be about as much indiscretion in preparing and outfitting now as there was in 1849. Nearly every company goes out loaded with guns, pistols and ammunition, and with provisions, clothing, and numerous little fixings, a large portion of which they will have to throw away between this and the mountains; and in the mean time they will have exhausted and broken down their teams and stock by their heavy loads.

When we visited Fort Laramie last summer, we found scattered along the road numerous valuable articles which had been abandoned; and beyond the Fort, we were well assured, it was still worse.

Emigrants going by land route are very apt to commit two errors. first they overload their teams at the start. Instead of limiting themselves to the *absolute necessaries* for a three month trip, they attempt to carry with them everything they think they may possible need, or which may add to the comforts and pleasure of the journey. In this way they overload their wagons, just at the time when the roads are soft and miry, and the streams generally high and the crossing difficult.

Then again, very many - we may safely say a majority - push their teams *too fast* at the outset. In their hurry and eagerness to get on, they drive further per day than they might. For, at the start, the animals have not learned to work properly together, neither have they yet been enured to subsisting on grass alone. Beside this, the early spring grass, especially to grain fed animals, is weakening. With an animal, as with a man, when the entire diet is changed, it requires time to adapt itself to the change.

Another thing emigrants should take notice of is the fact that the first part of the route is the worst, starting from anywhere on the Missouri River. There are more streams to cross, the banks are more precipitous, and there are incidents connected with the trip up to the crossing of the trip up to the crossing of the Platte, that make this end of the route trying on the teams and the travellers also. Those who husband their stock to this point will find profit in it.

With the number of emigrants going out, and the large amount of cattle which will be driven out, grass and water will, in may places, be scarce, if ti can be had at all. This will probably be particularly so in approaching the "South Pass and the Salt Lake Valley. Emigrants ought to be aware - and for this reason they may dispense with a great deal of their loads - that there are good large stores at Fort Kearny, fort Laramie, Fort Bridger and Salt Lake City.

At Forts Kearny and Laramie, the stock of all kinds of goods and provisions are very large, and any article can be procured that may be desired. The same is the case at Salk Lake city. Of the supply at Fort Bridger, we are not so fully informed. At Fort Laramie, we believe, the United States Government has a very large supply of provisions, which the commander ofhte post furnishes to emigrants at its cost to the Government. It is much better to pay the increase of prie than to injure the team by healing it over the Plains.

We have take the liberty of making these suggestions for the benefit of whom it may concern. we do not pretend to be correctly posted up as to all the preparations, outfit, and manner of traveling necessary for so long a journey as to California or Oregon, but our little experience last summer, and what we saw and learned from those who were familiar with those who were familiar with the Plains and the mountains, justify us in giving this much in the way of caution.

Properly prepared, with sufficient stock and wagons, not overloaded, and traveling at easy stages, we know of no trip that is more pleasant. The only mar is, that sometimes, in the cast plains, it becomes monotonous. The occasional necessity of forced marches furnishes variety and excitement to what would otherwise be a tedious journey.—*St. Louis Rep.*

X

ILLUSTRATIONS

Cover image
Oxen and Wagon. (n.d.) [Print]. Retrieved from http:/www.sorensenfamilyhistory.org/journey_west/corresp ondence_plains.htm.Sorensen Family History Organization. Web 17 Sep 2012.

Title page photo
Mary Alexander Casey Variel (1827-1907) photo from 1898 , Los Angeles; Retrieved from suesgreat8originally submitted this to Eaton Family Tree on 10 Mar 2011
http://trees.ancestry.com/tree/20888071/photo/2b1d3ee8-abbb-4fa4-a3c9-3d4e1e611825

Dedication photo
Joshua Hutchins Variel and Mary Alexander Casey Variel wedding portrait; Retrieved from suesgreat8originally submitted this to Eaton Family Tree on 14 Sep 2010 http://mediasvc.ancestry.com/ image/614b2f5c-fa57-443e-9b64-d87dd8cb8479.jpg?Client=Trees&NamespaceID=1093

1) New Harmony Indiana circa 1850 from the collection of Ian Donnachie Collection of Ian Donnachie. (n.d.) New Harmony, Indiana, circa 1850 [Print]. Retrieved from http://www.infed.org/images/places/new_harmony_print.jpg. The Encyclopaedia of Informal Education. Web. 09 Sep 2012.

2) Evansville, Indiana

Evansville, Indiana. (n.d.) [Print]. Retrieved from http://indianacatholic.mwweb.org/icath/wp-content/themes/wp-andreas03/img/front.jpg. Indiana Catholic History blog. Web. 20 Sep 2012.

3) St Louis Levee with Steamboats 1852
Steamboat Times
http://steamboattimes.com/images/levee_scenes/stlouis_levee1852thomas_easterly1600x1224.jpg

4) St. Joseph, Missouri
image from Oregon-California Trails Association courtesy of Courtesy of St. Joseph Museum. (n.d.) "Historic St. Joseph from Kansas." [Painting]. Retrieved from http://www.octa-trails.org/learn/virtual_trail/virtual_tour/st_joseph/index.php, Oregon-California Trails Association. Web. 07 Feb 2013

5) Early emigrant wagon train. (n.d.). [Photo]. Retrieved from http://www.spartacus.schoolnet.co.uk/WWwagontrain.htm. Spartacus Educational. Web. 05 Feb 2013.

6) Wagons crossing the plains. (n.d.) [Photo]. Retrieved from http://www.nps.gov/ciro/historyculture/historic-photos.htm. City of Rocks National Reserve Idaho. Web. 05 Feb 2013

7) Death on the trail (Drawing) Retrieved from National Oregon/California Trail center website, 09 February 2015, http://www.oregontrailcenter.org/HistoricalTrails/Dangers.htm; " The number of deaths which occurred in wagon train companies traveling to California is conservatively figured as 20,000 for the entire 2,000 miles of the Oregon/California Trail, or an average of ten graves per mile. "

8) Ferry - Lecompton Ferry over the Kansas River, Alexander Gardner, 1867. Legends of Kansas

http://www.legendsofkansas.com/lecompton.html
" Authority to establish a ferry across the Kansas River at Lecompton was granted by the Legislature, also in 1855. The same Legislature also incorporated the Lecompton Bridge Company, though no bridge was ever built. That same year, Lecompton was incorporated and designated as the county seat of Douglas County. The same Legislature also incorporated and permanently established the Kansas Medical College, at Lecompton, and appointed a board of fourteen Trustees. However, the college was never established."

9) View of Fort Kearney
http://cdrh.unl.edu/diggingin/historicimages/di.rg.2102.html; Diggin In: Historic Trails of Nebraska, University of Nebraska Lincoln, UNL Center for Digital Research in the Humanities

10) Wagons in a circle
http://www.usgennet.org/usa/ne/topic/ethnic/czechs/czpg33.html; US GenNet "The Vanguard of the Czech Pioneer´Drawing. n.d.

11) Ft. Laramie. (1849) [Drawing]. Sketch by James Wilkins. Retrieved from http://www.wyomingtalesandtrails.com/photosftlar.html. Fort Laramie Photos, Wyoming Tales and Trails. Web. 14 Oct 2012.

12) "Emigrant family fording the Platte." (n.d.) [Drawing]. Retrieved from http://tnspage.home.comcast.net/ ~tnspage/ThomasSmithNewFormat.htm#_Figure_25 A Glimpse at the Life and Times of Thomas Smith. Web. 19 Sep 2012.

13) Signatures at City of Rocks
Signatures at City of Rocks. (n.d.) [Photo} Retrieved from http://www.nps.gov/ciro/photosmultimedia/images/Emigr

ant-Signatures_1.JPG. City Of Rocks National Reserve Idaho. Web. 13 Oct 2012.

14) Yoke of oxen
"A Yoke of Oxen." F.N. Wilson. (1927) [Drawing]. Retrieved from http://www.lanecountyhistoricalsociety.org/Ox-Team_Days_on_the_Oregon_Trail.html. The Project Gutenberg eBook of Ox-Team Days on the Oregon Trail by Ezra Meeker. Web. 15 Oct 2012.

15) Letting down a wagon. F.N. Wilson. (1927) [Drawing]. Retrieved from http://www.lanecountyhistoricalsociety.org/Ox-Team_Days_on_the_Oregon_Trail.html. The Project Gutenberg eBook of Ox-Team Days on the Oregon Trail by Ezra Meeker. Web. 15 Oct 2012.

16) Camptonville - Yuba County 1850
Retrieved from http://books.google.com/books/download/The_Grizzly_Bear.pdf. "A Romance of the Plains" by Mary Alexander Variel, The Grizzly Bear, November 1907. Web. 29 Oct 2011.

17) Yuba Light Infantry in Camptonville, July 4, 1863. (1863) [Photo]. Retrieved from http://books.google.com/books/download/ The_Grizzly_Bear.pdf. "A Romance of the Plains" by Mary Alexander Variel, The Grizzly Bear, November 1907. Web. 29 Oct 2011.

18) *1878 Variel House, Plumas County, CA*; Retrieved 2013 from Plumas County, California, website; http://www.countyofplumas.com/index.aspx?NID=251

19) *Judge Robert Variel*, FindAGrave.com; Retrieved 2013 from http://www.findagrave.com/cgi-bin/fg.cgi?page= gr&GRid=73926667

20) *Joshua And Mary Variel And Family*

Tin Type of Joshua Variel (1816-1898) leaving Quincy for Los Angeles; Originally submitted to Easton Family Tree on 14 Sep 2010; Retrieved from http://trees.ancestry.com/tree/21290079 /person/5063474872/ media/2?pgnum =1&pg=0&pgpl=pid | pgNum

21) *Florence Variel, Daughter Of Joshua And Mary*
Originally submitted to Easton Family Tree 14 Sep 2010; Retrieved from http://trees.ancestry.com/tree/21290079/person/5063474872/media/2?pgnum=1&pg=0&pgpl=pid | pgNum

22) *Joshua Variel And Grandson Alexander*
Originally submitted to Easton Family Tree on 14 Sep; Retrieved from http://trees.ancestry.com/tree/21290079/person/5063474872/media/2?pgnum=1&pg=0&pgpl=pid | pgNum

23) *Robert And William Variel Iin Los Angeles Law Office*
Originally submitted to Easton Family Tree on 14 Sep 2010; Retrieved from http://trees.ancestry.com/tree/21290079/person/5063474872/media/2?pgnum=1&pg=0&pgpl=pid | pgNum

24) *Death notice of Joshua H. Variel*
From the front page of Los Angeles Herald, 4 March 1905. http://trees.ancestry.com/tree/20888071/person/1001413749/media/2?pgnum=1&pg=0&pgpl=pid | pgnum; Tsquare12 originally submitted this to Baldock family tree on 20 Jun 2011; Retrieved from ancestry.com 2013

CROSSING THE PLAINS

ABOUT THIS EDITION

This edition was made possible with the cooperation of the Variel family descendants, particularly Don Easton who has generously shared his family stories with the Camptonville History Society.

All maps and notes were created and compiled by Stephanie Korney, editor. Every attempt was made to provide accurate information,. For inadvertent errors, the editor apologizes.

Made in the USA
San Bernardino, CA
31 July 2017